The Essence of
Dṛk-Dṛśya Vivēka

Distinguishing the 'Perceiver' *from the* 'Perceived'

The Essence of
Dṛk-Dṛśya Vivēka

Distinguishing the 'Perceiver'
from the 'Perceived'

Sanskrit Text With Transliteration,
Translation and Index

Commentator
DR. SHRIKRISHNA D. DESHMUKH

Translator
MUKTA WALVEKAR

MOTILAL BANARSIDASS
SINCE 1903 IN INDOLOGY

First Edition : Delhi, 2018

ISBN : 978-81-208-4217-5

Also available at

MOTILAL BANARSIDASS

40-41 U.A. Bungalow Road, Jawahar Nagar, Delhi 110 007
1 B, J.S. Compound, Kennedy Bridge, Nana Chowk, Mumbai 400 007
203 Royapettah High Road, Mylapore, Chennai 600 004
236, 9th Main III Block, Jayanagar, Bengaluru 560 011
8 Camac Street, Kolkata 700 017
Ashok Rajpath, Patna 800 004
Chowk, Varanasi 221001

MLBD Cataloging-in-Publication Data

The Essence of
Dṛk-Dṛśya Vivēka: *Distinguishing the* 'Perceiver' *from the* 'Perceived'
by Dr. Shrikrishna D. Deshmukh
ISBN : 978-81-208-4217-5
I. Philosophy II. Vedanta III. Advaita
IV. Śaṅkarācārya V. Deshmukh, Shrikrishna D.
VI. Walvekar, Mukta

Published by

Motilal Banarsidass Publishers Private Limited
www.mlbd.com • mlbd@mlbd.com
Printed by Replika Press Pvt. Ltd.

Ādi Śaṅkarācārya

~ The Foremost Exponent of Advaita Vedānta ~

(788- 820 CE, Kaladi, Kerala)

Acknowledgement

Dṛk-Dṛśya Vivēka is an ancient treatise on Vedānta that delves deep into the nature of the Self. Working with this intriguing commentary has been a profound internal journey for me rather than just a job of translation.

I feel fortunate to be surrounded by many people who helped me along the way. *Dr. Jyotsna Patankar* and *Irina Derwall* did the intricate job of proofreading the translation and suggesting improvements in many places. *Tatiana Eremenko* provided us with the beautiful cover picture. *Mrs. Sonali Phadke* worked diligently to create the cover design that portrays the central theme of this treatise perfectly. *Mr. Pramod Walvekar* designed the book meticulously in the end. My sincere thanks to all of them!

I am deeply indebted to my revered Sadguru **Dr. Shrikrishna Deshmukh** for everything in life. This translation is only a result of his priceless guidance, gentle encouragement and supreme grace!

Mrs. Mukta Walvekar
(Translator)

Contents

Preface

Dṛk Dṛśya Vivēka is a composition of about 31 verses on the doctrine of Advaita Vedānta. Traditionally, it is believed to be authored by Ādi Śaṅkarācārya. Some scholars believe that it resembles texts such as Pañchadashi by Vidyāraṇya Swāmi. Either way, it is enough for seekers to believe that this text belongs to the tradition of Ādi Śaṅkarācārya.

There is a verse in Bṛihadāraṇyaka Upaniṣad -

न हि द्रष्टुर्दृष्टेः विपरिलोपो विद्यते ।

Na hi draṣṭurdṛuṣṭeḥ viparilopo vidyate / (4.3.23)

- 'The vision of the perceiver never ceases, since the perceiver is imperishable. Nothing is separate from the perceiver that can be perceived.'

This Śruti is the foundation of Dṛk-Dṛśya Vivēka.

The four key terms in this text are -

1. **Dṛk** (दृक्) - Ātman or Brahman or Sat-Cit-Ānanda i.e. (Pure) Existence, Consciousness, Bliss
2. **Draṣṭā** (द्रष्टा) - Jīva or embodied soul (perceiver or seer)
3. **Dṛṣṭi** (दृष्टी) - Eyes (sense organ for perceiving or seeing)
4. **Dṛśya** (दृश्य) - Perceivable world (gross and subtle objects that can be perceived or seen)

The perceiver acquires knowledge, which is of two kinds:

- Knowledge gained with sense organs or
- Knowledge pertaining to thoughts or feelings e.g. happiness, sorrow, jealousy, memories etc.

Vedānta says that every 'acquired knowledge' is based on the substratum of Pure Knowledge (Dṛk). Pure Knowledge exists eternally. It is independent of the triad of perceiver, perceivable and the organ of perception.

Jīva (embodied soul) believes that the world is real. Mumukṣu (मुमुक्षु, one who desires liberation), believes that Dṛk (Ātman) is real. Enlightened person realizes that the world is not real, only Dṛk is real. Enlightened person rejoices in the Pure Bliss of Ātman, Mumukṣu enjoys performing spiritual practices, while Jīva (worldly person) stays constrained in the mundane life full of dualities. Dṛk is eternal; while Draṣṭā, Dṛṣṭi and Dṛśya (perceiver, organ for perceiving and perceivable) are transient. Upaniṣad says -

रसो वै सः । *Raso vai saḥ* / (Tai. Up. 2.7)

- 'Brahman is the essence of the entire creation. It is full of the nectar of Bliss.'

Dṛk is verily the nectar of Pure Bliss. Only a tiny taste of it can be felt by Jīva through worldly objects. If a mango is peeled and juiced, its seed still carries the unique taste and aroma of the mango. Similarly, we get the glimpse of the Pure Bliss (of Brahman) while enjoying various objects and experiences in the world.

A discerning and inquisitive seeker instinctively feels the need to search for the origin of happiness that he finds in life. In the process, he gradually learns to discriminate between Dṛk and Dṛśya. This enquiry into 'the nature of eternal Dṛk and non-eternal Dṛśya', is the main subject of this treatise. A seeker with pure and calm mind, who is in search of eternal happiness, can discriminate in this manner.

There is a verse in Chāndogya Upaniṣad -

एकोऽहम् बहुस्याम् । *Eko'ham bahusyām* / (6.2.3)

- '(Brahman thinks) I am One and I shall manifest in many forms.'

The manifold Universe was created from this instinctive thought of Brahman. This is known as the theory of **false-attribution** (Adhyāropa, अध्यारोप). Brahman completely pervades the Universe, which is full of names and forms.

Ādi Śaṅkarācārya says -

अध्यारोपितनामरूपकर्मद्वारेण ब्रह्म निर्दिश्यते । (Bri. Up. 2.3.6)

Adhyāropita nāma rūpa karma dwāreṇa brahma nirdiśyate /

- 'We can infer the presence of Brahman whenever a name or a form or an activity is seen.'

Every entity has three aspects, which are -

- Existence (Asti, अस्ति)
- Cognizance (Bhāti, भाति)
- Likeable (Priya, प्रिय).

An entity 'exists', it is 'cognized', and it can be 'liked' or 'disliked'. Even though there is huge variation in names and forms, the three factors of existence, cognizance, and likeability are common amongst all of them. They are borrowed from the (Pure) Existence, Consciousness and Bliss (Sat, Cit, Ānanda) of Brahman. Brahman pervades everywhere in the world.

The treatise named Advaita Makaranda has a verse -

अहमस्मि सदा भामि कदाचिन्नाहमप्रियः ।

Ahamasmi sadā bhāmi kadachinnāhamapriyaḥ |

- 'I exist, I know my existence and I like myself.'

Every person can instinctively experience these three facts about himself. The instinct 'I exist' corresponds to Pure Existence, 'I know myself' corresponds to Pure Knowledge and 'I like myself' corresponds to Pure Bliss.

I exist	Pure Existence	Sat
I know myself	Pure Consciousness	Cit
I like myself	Pure Bliss	Ānanda

The three basic human instincts are borrowed from Sat-Cit-Ānanda i.e. Brahman. This underscores the fact that 'I am Brahman' i.e. 'I am (Pure) Existence,

Consciousness and Bliss.' Brahman (Dṛk) is the real nature of the Self or I.

Dṛk can be described as -

1. Birthless, deathless and ageless - in the context of sentience (Caitanya, चैतन्य)
2. Beginning-less, stateless and endless - in the context of insentience (Jaḍa, जड)
3. Perceiver, perceivable, perceiving - in the context of both sentience and insentience

Dṛk is Self-effulgent, while everything else is illumined by Dṛk.

The world (Dṛśya) can be broadly categorized in the following manner -

- **Empirical reality** (Vyāvahārika Sattā, व्यावहारिक सत्ता) - Entities with names and forms
- **Divine reality** (Īśvarī Sattā, ईश्वरी सत्ता), Existence, cognizance, likeable i.e. Asti, Bhāti, Priya
- **Absolute reality** (Pārmārthika Sattā, पारमार्थिक सत्ता) - Sat, Cit, Ānanda i.e. (Pure) Existence, Consciousness, Bliss

Ātman (Dṛk) does not perceive anything since it does not have any sense organ and action organ. The world (Dṛśya) does not perceive the perceiver. The eyes (Dṛṣṭi) do not perceive the perceiver and perceivable objects. It is Jīva (Draṣṭā), who perceives the world on the substratum of Dṛk with the help of eyes. However, Jīva does not realize the Knowledge of Dṛk due to ignorance (Ajñāna, अज्ञान).

Human life has two quintessential questions -

- Who am I? (Koham, कोहम्)
- How this world is formed? (Kathamidam jātam, कथमिदम् जातम्)

A seeker who constantly seeks answers to these two questions is naturally eligible (Adhikāri, अधिकारी) to study Dṛk-Dṛśya Vivēka. He should be inquisitive and have ability to discriminate between the real and unreal. Without proper discrimination, the study of this treatise could well just be an intellectual exercise.

Brahmasūtra says -

अथ अतः ब्रह्मजिज्ञासा । (1.1.1) *Atha ataḥ Brahmajijñāsā* |

- 'Therefore, now one (who is prepared) should inquire about Brahman.'

Muṇḍaka Upaniṣad says -

परीक्ष्य लोकान् कर्मचितान् ब्राह्मणो निर्वेदमायात् । (1.2.12)

Parikṣya lokān karmacitān brāhmaṇo nirvedamāyāt |

- 'A seeker should carefully examine the nature of the transient world gained by actions, reflect that nothing gained by Karma is eternal, and detach from the worldly life.'

This verse is the basis of the enquiry about the eternal Self (Dṛk) and the transient world (Dṛśya). Gross body and worldly objects constantly undergo changes such as creation, growth, decay and destruction. Some changes are favorable (Anukūla, अनुकूल), while some are not. What we desire takes place and what we don't desire also takes place. Similarly, what we dislike gets destructed and what we like gets destructed as well. This dual nature of life leads to happiness and misery. Favorite people, objects, events and circumstances do not lead to everlasting, Pure Bliss.

For aspirants of Pure Bliss, it is natural to feel inquisitive about the doctrine of Advaita Vedānta, which has been propounding Supreme and Pure Bliss of Brahman from ancient times. Ādi Śaṅkarācārya has made an unparalleled contribution to this tradition. All Maharashtrian saints have consistently propounded the same doctrine of Śāṅkarā Advaita Vedānta.

Life is filled with good and bad factors. Eternal Bliss cannot be found in a life oscillating between dualities. One should not stay emotionally attached to the mundane worldly life filled with dualities. Detachment is the main aspect of Nirveda i.e. renunciation (mentioned in the above verse). Without detachment, Dṛk (Pure Bliss) cannot be realized.

One who desires the Pure Bliss of Brahman can go on performing essential duties in life to some extent. At the same time, he should contemplate about Dṛk. The original meaning of the word Nirveda in the above verse means Asceticism (Sañyāsa, संन्यास). It is good if one can formally become a monk, and live life according to ascetic regulations. The path of formal Asceticism is obviously not meant for ordinary seekers.

However, one can think that 'I am not body, I am Pure Consciousness' while performing everyday tasks in a calm, composed manner. This is surely possible for many seekers. When basic responsibilities in life pertaining to education, family, job etc. are fulfilled, one should turn his complete focus towards the spiritual path.

Contemplating about Dṛk does not mean one should be aversive or resentful towards the surrounding world. One must live in his body, whether he is leading a worldly life or a spiritual life. Being happy, joyful and content is a very important part of human life. Aversion, antipathy or resentment bring in misery. With proper discrimination (Vivēka, विवेक), one can be convinced that all worldly entities are transient, while Dṛk, alone, is eternal. Vivēka enables the seeker to understand the insignificance of the world. Outward association with the world can be happily continued, while staying detached inside. Detachment results in a constant stream of internal happiness.

Vedānta states that, 'the world exists only so long as it is experienced, not otherwise'. This is the **Pratīti-**

mātra-Sattāvāna attribute of Māyā. Contemplating on this attribute enables the seeker to minimize his involvement in worldly matters and keep it limited to the basic necessities, which in turn helps to maintain a balanced outlook and brings enjoyment in life.

The world is full of beautiful, scenic aspects of nature, which rejuvenate the mind. Enjoying the Sun, the moon, stars, oceans, rivers, lakes, mountains, vallies and the sky is a great way to experience joy in life. Being with nature is usually a one-way relationship. E.g. the Sun is indifferent whether we like the Sunrise or not. The ocean doesn't react whether we feel joyous or scared looking at it. The mountain doesn't ask anyone to revisit it, irrespective of how much people enjoy it. Being in the company of neutral and scenic nature refreshes the mind.

Also, while treading the spiritual path, initially one can choose to be emotionally invested only in a handful of like-minded acquaintances, Sadguru and his favorite deity. Gradually, the investment in people can be minimized and one can contemplate on the teachings of saints and Sadguru.

As one evolves spiritually, he can experience what Lord Kṛṣṇa says in Bhagvad-Gītā -

आत्मन्येवात्मनोतुष्टः स्थितप्रज्ञस्तदोच्यते ।

Ātmanyevātmanotuṣhṭaḥ Sthitaprajñyastadocyate / (2.55)

- 'A person who finds satisfaction in the Self alone, is enlightened in real sense (Sthitaprajña, स्थितप्रज्ञ).'

The realization of Dṛk (Mokṣa or liberation) cannot be achieved with any worldly action. Even the most sublime, noble or enormous work does not lead to Mokṣa. Social work, donations, charity, generosity and service to the public has a great acceptance and recognition in the society. Selfless giving only helps to purify the mind, which in turn plays a big role in Self-realization.

Ādi Śaṅkarācārya firmly propounds -

वस्तुसिद्धिर्विचारेण न किंचित् कर्मकोटिभिः । (Vivekcūdāmaṇi.11)

Vastusiddhirvicāreṇa na kiṇcit-karma-koṭibhiḥ /

[Vastu means the Dṛk or Pure Consciousness.]

- 'The real nature of the Self is Dṛk. This can be realized only with deep contemplation. Millions of actions cannot lead to Self-realization.'

Bhagvad-Gītā has a verse which says -

लोकेऽस्मिन् द्विविधा निष्ठा ।

Loke'smin Dvividhā Niśṭhā / (3-3)

- 'One can choose to tread the 'path of knowledge' (Jñānaniśṭhā, ज्ञाननिष्ठा) or the 'path of action' (Karmaniśṭhā, कर्मनिष्ठा).'

Gītā doesn't mention worship (Upāsanā) as a separate third path in the spiritual journey. Worship is a type of action since it is consciously performed. Actions and worship are complementary to each other. Self-realization is the ultimate spiritual practice and experience.

The grace of Sadguru is considered imperative for the final stage of Self-realization. Incarnations like Rāma, Kṛṣṇa and saints such as Kabira, Jñāneśwara, and Tukārāma have clearly mentioned the significance of Sadguru in life. Some so-called scholars feel proud of their own brilliance and refuse to surrender to enlightened sages. Their ego is harmful for their own spiritual growth. Sadguru and disciple is not a mechanical relationship. Every disciple is an individual case, and Sadguru needs to mold him appropriately for further progress. Generic relationships between Guru and his disciples do not yield the desired results. Not many disciples evolve enough to get closer to the stage of Self-realization. But, every genuine disciple who comes to Sadguru should get appropriate guidance to progress on the spiritual path.

Dṛk (Brahman) is the only Eternal Truth (Satya, सत्य). Perceiver (Draṣṭā), perceived (Dṛśya) and the organ of perceiving (Dṛṣṭi) are all illusory in nature. Dṛk is 'Pure Knowledge' and Self-effulgent, while the other three (Draṣṭā, Dṛṣṭi and Dṛśya) get illumined by Dṛk. They can be known only in the light of Dṛk. Jīva (embodied soul) forgets his own nature, so he needs to perform spiritual practice for Self-realization. When Jīva realizes his true nature as Dṛk, the world (Dṛśya) becomes inconsequential for him.

Samādhi is a topic of great curiosity, amazement, astonishment and mysteriousness. There are stories of people sitting quietly in Samādhi for years together. Stories of Uddhava, Hanumāna in Samādhi are startling for many people. This treatise, however, explains the concept of Samādhi based on Vedānta philosophy in a lucid, coherent manner. Various types of Samādhi have been explained to help genuine seekers develop the firm belief that, they too can practice Samādhi. The success of this treatise indeed lies in this feature. This commentary is an attempt to study the text of Dṛk-Dṛśya Vivēka in detail with its nuances.

Dr. Shrikrishna D. Deshmukh

Murgud, Kolhapur

Foreword

The name of the text Dṛk-Dṛśya Vivēka suggests that it shows the difference between **Dṛk** (Ātman) and **Dṛśya** (दृश्य, the visible world). Vākya Sudha is another famous name for this treatise.

Logical intellect is the best tool to free the mind from incorrect ideas and conceptions. One who has logical intellect is rightly eligible for the study of Vedānta.

According to Vedānta, one must make use of his intellect for progressing on the path of Self-realization. The seeker's intellect should be as sharp as a razor's edge (क्षुरस्य धारा, *Kṣurasya Dhārā*, Katha Up.1.3.12 and 1.3.14) for treading on the spiritual path. The same intellect is called as Mahādhi or Mahābuddhi in Māṇḍūkya Kārikā (4.29).

Vedānta says that only the seeker who has righteous conduct, focused mind and controlled sense organs can realize Ātman with the help of subtle and sharp intellect (Katha Up. 1.2.24). The Knowledge of Ātman can be gained with meditation, pure intellect, persistent persuasion of the Eternal Truth and celibacy (Muṇḍaka. Up. 3.1.5).

Scholars have rightly understood the complexity of Vedānta doctrine and written many texts, treatises to supplement Vedānta philosophy. Such treatises are called as Prakaraṇa Grantha (प्रकरण ग्रंथ).

Dṛk-Dṛśya Vivēka is one such Prakaraṇa Grantha. Respected Swāmi Nikhilānanda from Rāmkrishna Matha has stated its significance in his commentary 'An inquiry into the nature of the Seer and the Seen'. The main purpose of this treatise is Self-realization with the practice of Samādhi. After realizing Ātman as the real Self, the enlightened person experiences (uninterrupted) Samādhi wherever his mind goes.

देहाभिमाने गलिते विज्ञाते परमात्मनि ।
यत्र यत्र मनो याति तत्र तत्र समाधयः ॥३०॥

Dehābhimāne galite vijñyāte Paramātmani |
Yatra yatra mano yāti tatra tatra Samādhayaḥ || 30 ||

- 'One who has detached himself from the body and achieved steady realization of Ātman as the real Self, experiences (uninterrupted) Samādhi wherever his mind is directed.'

Dr. Shrikrishna Deshmukh, who is a well-known saint from Kolhāpur District in Maharashtra, expressed a desire that I write a remark on his commentary on Dṛk-Dṛśya Vivēka. My association with Dr. Deshmukh goes back a long way. He has in-depth knowledge of the Upaniṣads and the Brahmasūtrās. He has done a phenomenal job of propounding the doctrine of Advaita Vedānta in lucid language through his many lectures, discourses and writings. His work continues even today, and I feel short at words to express appreciation for his contribution to the field.

Dr. Deshmukh has cited many scholarly references in this text. His profound knowledge and distinguished writings are highly remarkable. I pray to the God for his long healthy life, so he can continue his work of propounding the Advaita Vedānta doctrine.

Iti Sham!

Swami Bhaumanandaji Maharaj

Former President (Ramkrishna Matha, Pune.)

Introduction

Bhagvad-Gītā gives us valuable guidance in this highly inspiring verse:

ये हि संस्पर्शजा भोगा दुःखयोनय एव ते ।
आद्यन्तवन्तः कौन्तेय न तेषु रमते बुधः ॥

Ye hi saṁsparśajā bhogā duḥkhayonaya eva te |
Ādyantavantaḥ Kaunteya na teṣu ramate budhaḥ || (5-22)

- 'Pleasures arising from the contact of senses with sense objects are indeed a source of misery, since they are subject to a beginning and an end. O Arjuna! Intelligent and discriminative people do not take delight in worldly pleasures or stay attached to them.'

Dṛk-Dṛśya Vivēka is a treatise meant for discerning, qualified people. It is believed that either Ādi Śaṅkarācārya or Śri Bhārati Tīrtha or Śri Vidyāraṇya Swāmi has authored this treatise. Irrespective of who the real author is, this is an excellent commentary that outlines the difference between eternal and non-eternal aspects of life (Ātman and Anātman).

Dr. Shrikrishna Deshmukh, who is a learned scholar in the doctrine of Advaita Vedānta and a faithful follower of the teachings of saints, has beautifully unveiled the gist of this treatise. Vedānta propounds the use of accurate logic with Vivēka i.e. discrimination between real and unreal aspects of life. The theory of Vedānta explains the transient nature of the body, the mind and the intellect. It teaches consistent contemplation of the non-dual principle of Brahman. This treatise on Advaita Vedānta has 31 verses in total. The states of waking and dream are permeated with names and forms. They are delusively perceived to be real due to the veiling power (Āvaraṇa Śakti, आवरण शक्ति) and projecting power (Vikṣepa Śakti, विक्षेप शक्ति) of Māyā, which hide Ātman or Dṛk. The author has provided references from Upaniṣads and Smritis (Bhagvad-Gītā etc.) to systematically explain the fact that the veil on Dṛk can be removed and powers of Māyā can be rendered ineffective. This is the characteristic feature of his commentary.

All the sense experiences (seeing, hearing etc.) take place on the substratum of Ātman. However, ordinary people and many scholars cannot discern this fact. Ātman transcends both the experience and the experiencer. We experience the three states of waking, dream and deep-sleep every day. Worldly experiences are based on the dualistic mindset, e.g. 'I and mine', 'enjoyer and objects of enjoyment' etc. The duality of 'I and mine' binds us in the waking as well as the dream state. The 'I' that experiences various events in dreams, is the same 'I' that experiences completely different events in the waking state. The events in dreams are regarded as unreal once we get up. Similarly, joys and sorrows in the waking state become inconsequential in deep-sleep. In deep-sleep, the mind and the intellect stop working and one cannot hear anything even though ears are open. But after waking up, one says that 'I had a very sound sleep'.

We assume that the triad of perceiver-perceived-perceiving (Draṣṭā- Dṛśya-Darśana, द्रष्टा-दृश्य-दर्शन) is real. However, the triad of the perceiver, perceived, and perceiving dissolves in the deep-sleep. Jīva (embodied soul) becomes one with Ātman (Pure Consciousness). Jīva experiences the highest, unparalleled Pure Bliss and receives great energy in deep-sleep. In the waking state, Jīva perceives his own body and all other objects as separate from each other due to the 'projecting power' (Vikṣepa Śakti, विक्षेपशक्ति) of Māyā. The author has explained this in his commentary on verses 10-19. The world and all worldly activities are based on the theory of 'false attribution' (Adhyāropa, अध्यारोप) and 'false superimposition' (Adhyāsa, अध्यास). When a rope is delusively perceived as a snake in dusk, the snake is neither real nor unreal. In fact, the snake has no existence at any time. Similarly, the visible world has no factual existence at any time, it is only a delusive perception on the substratum of Ātman.

Ādi Śaṅkarācārya says in his Dakshinā Mūrti Stotra-

विश्वं पश्यति कार्यकारणतया स्वस्वामिसम्बन्धतः ।
शिष्याचार्यतया तथैव पितृपुत्राद्यात्मना भेदतः ।

स्वप्ने जाग्रति वा य एष पुरुषो मायापरिभ्रामितः ।

तस्मै श्रीगुरुमूर्तये नम इदं श्रीदक्षिणामूर्तये ॥ 8 ॥

Viśvaṃ paśyati kāryakāraṇatayā svasvāmi-Saṃbandhataḥ |

Shishyāchāryatayā tathaiva pitṛputrādyātmanā bhedataḥ ||

Svapne jāgrati vā ya eṣa puruṣo Māyāparibhrāmitaḥ

Tasmai Śrī Gurumūrtaye nama idam Śri Dakshiṇāmūrtaye ||

- 'The differences that we see in the world as cause and effect, servant and master, teacher and disciple, father and son etc. are all differentiations in one Ātman. These differences in the dream and the waking state are created by the indescribable (Anirvachaniya, अनिर्वचनीय) power of Māyā.'

Ādi Śaṅkara firmly propounds that all these experiences are transient, changeable, relative, bound to end, non-permanent and illusory (Mithyā, मिथ्या) in nature. They cannot be considered as real (Satya, सत्य).

These experiences are relative to the daily life of an individual because the mind (Manas, मन), intellect (Buddhi, बुद्धि), memory (Citta, चित्त) and ego (Ahaṅkāra, अहंकार) are illumined by Ātman or the Witness (Sākṣī). The intellect can understand and learn new things in the light of Ātman. The light of Ātman is not the same as the worldly light emitted by the Sun or the fire. It is divine in nature. It is (Pure) Existence, Consciousness and Bliss (Sat, Cit, Ānanda). Names and forms belong to the empirical world (Vyāvahārika Sattā, व्यावहारिक सत्ता).

Ātman is the only One, permanent, eternal and non-dual principle. But due to the inconceivable power of Māyā, it is wrongly identified with the changing and transient entities in the world.

How do we eradicate the power of Māyā and ignorance (Ajñāna)? Lord Kṛṣṇa has earnestly guided us with spiritual practices for surrendering to Īśvara in Bhagvad-Gītā for the same purpose.

तस्मात् सर्वेषु कालेषु माम् अनुस्मर युध्य च ।

Tasmāt sarveṣu kāleṣu mām anusmara yudhya ca | (8-22)

- 'Therefore, Arjuna, think of Me at all times and perform your prescribed duty of fighting.'

मय्येव मन आधत्स्व मयि बुद्धिं निवेशय ।

Mayyeva mana ādhatsva mayi Buddhin niveśaya | (12-8)

- 'Fix your mind on Me alone and think of Me alone.'

मामेव ये प्रपद्यन्ते मायामेतां तरन्ति ते ।

Māmeva ye prapadyante māyāmetāḿ taranti te | (7-14)

- 'Only those who wholeheartedly surrender to me, are able to surmount the illusory power of Māyā.'

From the 20th to 25th verse, there is guidance on how to eradicate ignorance with the theory of false attribution and subsequent invalidation of the same (Adhyāropa-Apavāda, अध्यारोप - अपवाद). Dr. Shrikrishna Deshmukh has explained these verses in a very lucid, forthright manner.

His commentary helps seekers to contemplate deeper, focus more and enhance their spiritual practice.

The topic of Dṛk-Dṛśya Vivēka can be discerned only with the subtle intellect (Sūkṣma Buddhivṛtti, सूक्ष्म बुद्धिवृत्ती). There is a verse in Katha Upaniṣad that says -

दृश्यते त्वग्रया बुद्ध्या सूक्ष्मया सूक्ष्मदर्शिभिः । (1.3.12)

Dṛśyate tvagryayā buddhyā sūkṣmayā sūkṣmadarśibhiḥ|

- 'Only the subtle seers can realize Ātman through their sharp and subtle intellect.'

One should remember this fact, follow guidance of Sadguru and continue studying scriptures. Consistent hearing and contemplation about Ātman eventually leads the seeker to Self-realization.

St. Jñāneśwara says in his text Anubhavāmṛut that the perceiver is not separate from the perceived objects. They are essentially the same. He further says in his text Chāṅgadeva Pāsaṣti that the process of pure perception, where the perceiver is not separate from the perceived, is the very nature of Self-realization. In general, perception means experiencing the world with sense organs. But the realization of Ātman is completely different from the general process of perception.

Māṇḍūkya Upaniṣad calls this as **Turiya** (तुरीय). In the context of Turiya, all experiences in the waking state are illusory (Mithyā). Turiya is also known as Brahman,

Ātman, Dṛk, Pure Consciousness or the Witness Consciousness (Sākṣī Caitanya, साक्षी चैतन्य). The same thing has been addressed by Bhagvad-Gītā in the verse -

निष्ठाज्ञानस्य या परा ।

Niśṭhājñānasya yā parā (18.50)

- '(Realization of Ātman is) the Supreme state of Knowledge.'

St. Gaudpādācārya has written the following verse for Pure Consciousness or Dṛk -

अस्पर्शयोगो वै नाम दुर्दर्शः सर्वयोगिभिः । (Māṇḍūkya Kārikā 3.39)

Asparśayogo vai nāma durdarśaḥ sarvayogibhiḥ /

- 'Realization of Ātman, which cannot be touched (since it is non-dual), is hard to experience even for all Yogis.'

This text is an effort to pen down the experience of Nirvikalpa Samādhi. Swāmi Vivekānanda says in one of his lectures -

'The entire world will be seen in the new light. We will see the world in a very different form. When we see the world, we will also know that it is not real the way it seems. We will never forget the difference between a mirage and real water.'

From 26th to 30th verse in this book, there is a detailed description of Samādhi. Dr. Shrikrishna Deshmukh has used the following definition of Samādhi for this text.

समाधियते यस्मिन् अंतःकरणं इति समाधिः ।

Samādhiyate yasmin Antaḥkaraṇam iti Samādhiḥ /

- 'One whose mind is completely absorbed (in Brahman) is said to be in Samādhi.'

While reading this commentary on Samādhi, readers can evidently understand that the author has written it based on his own experience. Some of the statements are truly engaging. E.g. 'Samādhi cannot be experienced in a limited or a single body part. Some Sampradāyas ask to establish focus in middle of the eyebrows, tip of the nose, center of the heart etc., which is fine in their own context. This text does not refute that. Some people see dazzling light, hear mystic sound (Anāhata nāda, अनाहत नाद), or experience their body growing exceptionally tall in the preliminary stages of Samādhi. That might be encouraging or motivating for practitioners. Some may feel scared of disconnecting from the physical body (death) before attaining the final stage of Samādhi. But such fear should be resolutely discarded. Jīva (embodied soul) leaves the body only according to his destiny (Prārabdha, प्रारब्ध). E.g. before sleeping, it is meaningless to feel skeptical about whether one would wake up from sleep. It is equally meaningless to feel anxious about whether one would actually come out of Samādhi before entering into it.' The author has given highly useful guidance to all discerning and sharp readers. The text does not have intellectual gymnastics, nor does it confuse or disorient the readers.

Here I remember a story narrated by Śri Rāmkrishna. He said, 'Once a doll made up of salt went inside an ocean to measure it. She was planning to measure the depth of the water. But the moment she stepped inside the ocean, she got dissolved into the water completely'.

Seers have said in Śvetāśvetara Upaniṣad -

न संदृशे तिष्ठति रूपमस्य, न चक्षुषा पश्यति कश्चनैनम् ।
हृदा हृदिस्थं मनसा य एनम्, एवं विदुरमृतास्ते भवन्ति ॥

Na sandṛśe tiṣṭhati rūpamasya |
Na chakṣuṣā paśyati kaścanainam |
Hṛdā hṛdistham manasā ya enam |
Evam viduramṛtāste bhavanti || (4-20)

There is a similar verse in Katha Upaniṣad:

न संदृशे तिष्ठति रूपमस्य, न चक्षुषा पश्यति कश्चनैनम् ।
हृदा मनीषा मनसाभिक्लृप्तो, य एतद्विदुरमृतास्ते भवन्ति ॥

Na sandṛśe tiṣṭhati rūpamasya |
Na chakṣuṣā paśyati kaścanainam |
Hṛdā manīṣā manasābhiklrupto |
Ya etat viduramṛtāste bhavanti || (3-9)

Both these verses mean the same -

- 'This (formless) Ātman cannot be realized with the sight. It cannot be seen with the eyes. This Ātman can only be comprehended with the pure, subtle and calm intellect. Those, who realize that Ātman is Brahman, become eternal in essence.'

In Dṛk-Dṛśya Vivēka, Ātman is termed as Dṛk. The main topic of Dṛk-Dṛśya Vivēka is the same as those of Upaniṣads. Turiyā Ātman is the same as Dṛk. Seekers get a platform for broad, comprehensive thinking with the help of profound texts such as these.

Dr. Deshmukh, who is a distinguished spiritual author, brings in great depth and subtlety to the thinking process of seekers. His lucid commentary on Dṛk-Dṛśya Vivēka is a precious addition to the set of Vedānta treatises.

Swami Brahmasthanandaji Maharaj
President (Ramkrishna Math, Dhantoli, Nagpur)

The Essence of

Dṛk-Dṛśya Vivēka

The Essence of Dṛk-Dṛśya Vivēka

Perceived and Perceiver

रूपं दृश्यं लोचनं दृक् तद् दृश्यं दृक् तु मानसम् ।
दृश्या धीवृत्तयः साक्षी दृगैव न तु दृश्यते ॥ १ ॥

Rūpaṃ dṛśyaṃ locanaṃ dṛk tad dṛśyam dṛk tu mānasaṃ |
Dṛśyā dhīvrittayaḥ sākṣī dṛgaiva na tu dṛśyate || 1 ||

Meaning: The form (rūpa, रूप) is perceived and the eye is the perceiver. The eye itself is perceived and the mind is its perceiver (mind with Reflected Consciousness i.e. Cidābhāsa, चिदाभास). The mind is perceived and the Witness (Sākṣī, साक्षी) is its perceiver. But the Witness (Sākṣī or Ātman) cannot be perceived by anything else.

Eye is considered as a representative of all other sense organs. The eye is (as if) tied to a form. Everything in the field of vision is involuntarily seen when eyes are opened. Similarly, all sense organs perceive their respective objects (e.g. nose smells, ears hear etc.). Sense organs, by themselves, are insentient (Jaḍa, जड) in nature. They belong to Jīva (embodied soul). Jīva cannot perceive anything with sense organs unless the mind with Reflected Consciousness (Cidābhāsa, चिदाभास) is attached to the organs. E.g. in deep-sleep, Jīva does not see or perceive anything because the mind is dissolved at that time.

Everything that is known or learnt by Jīva is called as 'perceivable form' or 'object' (**Dṛśya**, दृश्य). Seeing (perceiving) and knowing are two different processes. Everything that is 'seen or perceived' is not necessarily 'known' at the same time.

- **Seeing** - All objects are 'seen or perceived' in the light of the Sun, the moon or a lamp.
- **Knowing** - However, all objects are 'known' in the divine light, which is the light of Self-effulgent Ātman.

Ātman is the ultimate perceiver, as no other perceiver is known to exist that can perceive Ātman. It is also known as Pure Consciousness or Dṛk (दृक्). Jīva perceives all objects in the light of Ātman (Ātmaprakāśa, आत्मप्रकाश). When happiness or sadness is 'felt' in the light of Ātman, the same Ātman is called as the Witness (Sākṣī, साक्षी).

Self-effulgent Ātman cannot see (know) anything that gets illumined by its own light, since Ātman is eyeless as stated in Muṇḍaka Upaniṣad. Bṛihadāraṇyak Upaniṣad reiterates the same fact -

केन किं विजानीयात् ।

Ken kim vijāniyāt | (4.5.15)

- '(In the non-dual realm of Ātman) who can possibly know whom?'

The process of 'illumining objects' is just a language of false attribution (Adhyāropa, अध्यारोप). In reality, objects that can be illumined (known) do not exist. Jīva (embodied soul) delusively perceives them to be real. Objects are neither created by eyes nor by Ātman. They are only believed to have perceptual existence in the Empirical Reality (Vyāvahārika Sattā, व्यावहारिक सत्ता).

One Sense Organ can see Many Forms

नील – पीत – स्थूल – सूक्ष्म - ह्रस्वदीर्घादि भेदतः ।
नानाविधानि रूपाणि पश्येल्लोचनमेकधा ॥ २ ॥

Nīla pīta sthūla sūkṣma hraswadīrghādi bhedataḥ |
Nānāvidhāni rūpāṇi paśyellocanamekadhā || 2 ||

Meaning: The eye is essentially only one sense organ (even if there are two), but it perceives various forms (objects of perception) such as gross, subtle, short, long etc., and colors as yellow, blue etc.

Differentiation in colors (blue, yellow), sizes (short, long) and measurements (length, height) are seen by only one eye organ. All objects, however different, belong to only one category of perceived (Dṛśya, दृश्य). From the perspective of all objects, their perceiver is only one i.e. the eye. Even if there are many distinctions in objects, number or type of eyes need not be many to see them separately.

The Same Rule Applies to the Mind and Other Organs

आन्ध्यमान्द्यपटुत्वेषु नेत्रधर्मेषु चैकधा ।
संकल्पयेन्मनः श्रोत्रत्वगादौ योज्यतामिदम् ॥ ३ ॥

Āndhyamāndya paṭutweṣu netradharmeṣu caikadhā |
Sañkalpayenmanaḥ shrotratwagādau yojyatāmidam || 3 ||

Meaning: Blindness, dull vision or very sharp vision are characteristics of eyes which are perceived only by the mind. Same is the case with objects perceived by other sense organs such as ears, skin etc.

The mind consists of the wind element and Rajoguṇa. It is insentient (Jaḍa, जड) in nature, but it becomes capable of acquiring knowledge due to the presence of Cidābhāsa i.e. Reflected Consciousness in it. Just as light permeates completely in a clear glass prism, Pure Consciousness (the light of Ātman) permeates in the mind. When Pure Consciousness reflects or permeates in the mind, it is called as '**Reflected Consciousness**' or **Cidābhāsa**.

Even though the eye is the perceiver of many objects (as mentioned in verse 2), the eye itself is perceived by the mind. Changes in the eye (vision) are known only to the mind. It is mind that thinks 'I am blind, or I have dull vision, or I am unable to see'. No separate eyes are needed to see (know) the different characteristics of eyes such as blindness, dullness etc. Same is the case with other sense organs. The ears, the skin etc. are perceivers of their respective objects, yet they themselves are perceived only by the mind.

Perception by the five sense organs lead to dual experiences -

1. Ears - Words (Appreciation and criticism)
2. Skin - Touch (Hot and cold)
3. Eye - Form (Beautiful and ugly)
4. Tongue - Taste (Delicious, tasteless)
5. Nose - Smell (Aromatic and stinky)

Jīva (embodied soul) becomes happy or sad when dealing with these dualities. He does not experience the stream of constant, eternal Bliss as his life oscillates between joy and misery. But Dṛk (Pure Consciousness) is eternally calm as mentioned in Māṇḍūkya Kārika-

प्रपंचोपशम शान्तं । (1.7)

Pranpañchopśama Śāntaṃ /

- 'Ātman (Dṛk) is cessation of the phenomenal world. It is eternal peace.'

Dṛk pervades all perceivable objects yet remains detached from them. Dṛk illumines all organs, their respective objects and the intellect (Buddhi, बुद्धि). Dṛk is the real 'I' or 'Self'. The supreme, eternal Bliss can be experienced only when sentient (Cetan, चेतन) Dṛk is seen (realized) separately from the insentient objects.

The Mind and Its Traits get Illumined by Dṛk

कामः संकल्पसंदेहौ श्रद्धाऽश्रद्धे धृतीतरे ।

ह्रीर्धीर्भीरित्येवमादीन् भासयत्येकधा चितिः ॥ ४ ॥

Kāmaḥ sañkalpa sandehau śraddhā'śraddhe dhṛtītare |

Hrīrdhīrbhīrityevamādin bhāsayatyekadhā citiḥ || 4 ||

Meaning: (Traits of the mind such as) Desires, resolves, doubts, faith, skepticism, grit, modesty, understanding, fear are illumined by only one Pure Consciousness.

Dṛk illumines everything that is perceivable (knowable). Kena Upaniṣad clearly explains the same principle –

प्रतिबोध विदितं मतं अमृतत्वं हि विन्दते । (2.4)

Pratibodha viditaṃ mataṃ amṛtatvaṃ hi vindate |

- 'Every 'acquired knowledge' is based on the substratum of 'Pure Knowledge' (Jñanrūpa Ātman, ज्ञानरूप आत्मा), which is eternally present. Even if no new knowledge is acquired from outside, Dṛk i.e. Pure Knowledge exists at all times.'

Desires in the mind get manifested in various forms such as hope, wish, expectation, aspiration, craving etc. Excessive attachment, greed and daydreaming are the effects of desires. Subconscious imprints (Vāsanā) bring out desires in the mind. Every desire is rooted in 'craving for happiness'. One craves for happiness from external objects due to the ignorance of the Knowledge of Dṛk (Ātman), which is the ever-available, internal Bliss. Desires, cravings and ignorance are all known by Jīva (embodied soul) in the light of Self-effulgent Dṛk. The feasibility or usefulness of fulfilling a desire is illumined by Dṛk. Craving for unattainable desires is understood in the light of Dṛk itself. The fact that 'I am unable to fulfill a desire' or 'I should strive for fulfilling a desire' is known in the light of Dṛk as well. All these states of the mind ultimately point to Dṛk.

Many resolutions emerge in the mind to fulfill the pending desires. There is a verse which says -

यो यदिच्छसि तस्य तत् । (Katha. Up. 1.2.16)

Yo yadicchasi tasya tat |

- 'Every desire gets fulfilled in due course of time in one or the other form (as per Īśvara's system).'

Hence, seekers should cultivate desires pertaining to eternal Bliss and move away from worldly desires.

New resolutions emerge due to three reasons –

- Ignorance of ever-available, Pure Bliss of Ātman
- Illusion that the 'world is real'
- Expectation of happiness from people or objects

However, completion of resolutions is constrained by destiny (Prārabdha, प्रारब्ध). Ignorance of these constraints leads to resistance towards the law of Karma established by Īśvara. This entire knowledge is understood by Jīva in the light of Self-effulgent Dṛk. Beneficial or harmful traits (for spiritual pursuit) are comprehended in the same light of Dṛk. 'Dṛk itself is the eternal, Pure Bliss', once this is clearly understood, all resolutions and desires for worldly happiness automatically subside and wear away.

Human life is filled with doubts, skepticism, apprehensions, distrust, delusions, hesitancy and uncertainty. Strong likings, dis-likings and mood swings get added to that. All these mental states are illumined by Dṛk. In the complex web of human emotions, the illuminator (Prakāśaka, प्रकाशक) Dṛk gets completely sidelined and illumined emotions (Prakāśya, प्रकाश्य) grab all the attention. Vedic scriptures help us appropriately discriminate between these two. If the scriptures are learnt and put into practice, we will be able to contemplate about Dṛk in a constant manner.

Human intellect is tainted with four types of faults:

1. Illusion (Bhrama, भ्रम)
2. Blunder (Pramāda, प्रमाद)

3. Imperfect senses (Karaṇāpātava, करणापाटव)
4. Excessive greed (Vipralipsā, विप्रलिप्सा)

By itself, the mind is incapable of being decisive about where the real welfare lies. Hence it is beneficial to quietly follow the path shown by enlightened seers and scriptures, discard all apprehensions and stay in reflective connection with Dṛk (Ātmanusandhāna, आत्मानुसंधान).

Faith and skepticism, both get illumined by Dṛk. Being a believer and nurturing faith is an immensely important trait. A genuine seeker should make utmost use of the human body that he is born with. He may surely invest some time in earning basic necessities of life, but not run behind worldly luxuries. Contemplating on 'who am I' should be the fundamental quest of human life, which involves treading the spiritual path. In spiritual pursuit, one should establish unwavering faith on Īśvara, saints, Sadguru, Śruti, Smruti and commentaries on them. Righteous behavior needs to be embraced in both spiritual and everyday life. Life spent faithfully in accordance with these values generally continues in an uneventful manner. The impact of worldly matters (Dṛśya, दृश्य) gradually starts receding. Dṛk can be deeply contemplated in peaceful environment. The human life can be utilized in its entirety this way.

Skeptic mindset is prevalent since ancient Vedic era. The fact that 'I am a skeptic' also gets discerned in the light of Dṛk. Ātman is the ultimate topic for the faith. Ignorance about Ātman or Knowledge of Ātman gets illumined by Dṛk itself. Blind faith practices proliferate in the light of Dṛk as well. They should be discarded as and when they are discerned. Detached mindset evolves from faithfulness. People who spend many hours in the tiny, enclosed cabins of space shuttles or submarines require an unusual mindset, which needs to be developed under simulated conditions. Similarly, people who nurture detachment by staying in remote caves or basements have a different mindset. St. Tukārāma Mahārāja sung bhajans on an open hilltop while St. Gahinināth spent much of his life meditating in caves. They are both at par in terms of their faith, commitment and detachment. Both practiced the same goal of realization of Dṛk and both their mindsets can be comprehended in the light of Dṛk.

Dhṛti means fortitude. Decisiveness, tenacity, resilience are its manifestations. Everyone has these traits in varying degrees. Both fearful nature and brave nature get discerned in the light of Dṛk. Instead of mocking meekness in a person or admiring his bravery, the substratum of Dṛk should be contemplated with utmost focus.

Dṛk evenly illumines all traits of the mind such as being good, bad, moral, immoral, pious, sinful, righteous, non-righteous, decent, indecent, cultured, non-cultured etc. Seeker should learn to focus on Dṛk instead of getting carried away with the oscillations in the mind.

Eternal Dṛk that Illumines Everything Else

> नोदेति नास्तमेत्येषा न वृद्धिं याति न क्षयम् ।
> स्वयं विभात्यथान्यानि भासयेत् साधनं विना ॥ ५ ॥

Nodeti nāstyametyeṣa na vriddhiṃ yāti na kṣayam |
Swayaṃ vibhātyathānyāni bhāsayet sādhanaṃ vinā || 5 ||

Meaning: This (Dṛk or Pure Consciousness) does neither rise nor set. It neither grows nor decays. Being Self-effulgent in nature, it illuminates everything else without any other aid.

There are many known forms of emerging - the Sun rises, the world manifests, Jīva (embodied soul) takes birth, Īśvara takes incarnation, milk gets converted into curd etc. But, Dṛk (Pure Consciousness) does not emerge or rise in any of these ways. It exists eternally in the form of Sat. It transcends time.

Dṛk is -

- **Anādi** (अनादि) - Beginning-less
- **Ādya** (आद्य) – Primordial, the very first, earliest existence.
- **Satya** (सत्य) - Absolute Truth, time-transcendental. Exists in all three times of past, present and future.

- **Nitya** (नित्य) - Eternal. It exists everywhere, equally, at all times.

An object can be non-existent in one of the four ways:

1. **Prior non-existence** (Prāgabhāva, प्राक् अभाव) - Non-existence (of an object) before creation.
2. **Posterior non-existence** (Pradhvamsābhāva, प्रध्वंसा अभाव) - Non-existence (of an object) following destruction.
3. **Absolute non-existence** (Atyantābhāva, अत्यंता अभाव) - Absolute non-existence in all times. E.g. Thorns of a hare.
4. **Mutual non-existence** (Anyonyābhāva, अन्योन्य अभाव) is absence of one entity in the other and vice-versa. E.g. a flower is absent in a fruit and vice versa.

Dṛk is the eternal, transcendental truth (Satya, सत्य). It cannot be non-existent in any of the above four ways.

Dṛk is also referred to as the most ancient or primeval (Ādya, आद्य). One that does not manifest cannot possibly wane. One that isn't born cannot die. Gross body, which is insentient (Jaḍa, जड) in nature, dies or gets destroyed. Dṛk does not ever set (disappear), like the Sun or the moon.

Any entity can be destroyed in three ways. Dṛk is not destroyed in any of the three possible ways -

1. **Svataḥ Nāśa** (स्वतः नाश) - Dṛk does not get destroyed automatically by itself.
2. **Parataḥ Nāśa** (परतः नाश) - Dṛk cannot be destroyed by any other entity, since it is the only One non-dual principle.
3. **Aśraya Nāśa** (आश्रयनाश) - In some cases, an object gets wiped out when its shelter comes to an end. E.g. a flower on a tree is automatically destroyed when the tree itself is crushed. But Dṛk does not get destroyed due to destruction of its shelter.

The process of growth and decay takes place in all objects with forms. Dṛk is formless, so it neither grows nor decays. Every object undergoes six modifications in its lifetime -

1. Birth (Jāyate - जायते)
2. Existence (Asti - अस्ति)
3. Growth (Vardhate - वर्धते)
4. Change (Vipariṇamate - विपरिणमते)
5. Decay (Apakṣīyate - अपक्षीयते)
6. Death (Mriyate - म्रियते)

Dṛk does not undergo any of these modifications. Dṛk (Ātman or Pure Consciousness) is completely detached from modifications in the body. Dṛk does not have 'perceivable existence' i.e. name and form. It also does not have 'absolute non-existence' as stated above.

Dṛk is Self-effulgent (Swayaṃprakāśa, स्वयंप्रकाश). It is Self-luminous and eternally-shining. It is Pure Knowledge, which exists irrespective of the knower or knowable. It is 'Self-cognizant' (Swasaṃvedya, स्वसंवेद्य) i.e. one that cannot be comprehended by routine means of gaining knowledge but can be cognized only by being One with it. It is eternally-attained (Nityaprāpta, objective (Vastutantra, वस्तुतंत्र) and eternally-existent (Nityasiddha, नित्यसिद्ध). The words Ātman, Brahman or Dṛk denote the same Pure Consciousness, which transcends the concept of time, gender and three Guṇās (Sattva, Rajas and Tamas).

There is a Sanskrit verse which says -

दृक् साधनं विना अन्यानि भासयेत् ।

Dṛk sādhanaṃ vinā anyāni bhāsayet |

- 'Dṛk illumines all other entities without using any aid such as sense organs.'

Katha Upaniṣad reiterates the same fact -

तमेव भान्तं अनुभाति सर्वं तस्य भासा सर्वमिदं विभाति ।

Tameva bhāntaṃ anubhāti sarvaṃ |

Tasya bhāsā sarvamidaṃ vibhāti || (5-15)

- 'The self-luminous light of Ātman i.e. Pure Knowledge, is the main reason why every knowable entity is known by the knower.'

In reality, knower who is separate from the Pure Knowledge does not exist. (Nānyat kopi draṣṭā - नान्यत् कोपि द्रष्टा).

The relationship of illuminator (Dṛk) and illuminable (Dṛśya) is imaginary, since every perceived entity is imaginary. In everyday life, eyes see objects in the light emitted by the Sun and the moon. But these sources of light do not exist separately in Brahman. They themselves get illumined (known) due to the effulgence of Dṛk (Ātmaprakāśa, आत्मप्रकाश). No separate light is needed to see the light of the Sun, the moon etc. Similarly, no other aids for knowledge are needed to know Ātman, which is Pure Knowledge itself. Eyes only 'see' an object in the empirical light of the Sun and the moon. But the process of 'knowing' the object only takes place in the divine and eternal light of Ātman.

Even the ignorance that 'Ātman does not exist' becomes 'known' in the light of Ātman itself. Ignorance (Ajñāna, अज्ञान) is not the opposite of Knowledge (Jñāna, ज्ञान). Ignorance means that, which obstructs the process of realization of Pure Knowledge. Ignorance is the result of illusion that the world exists for real. Ignorance about the nature of the Self and the world gets eradicated in the light of Dṛk, when Sadguru (Spiritual Master) bestows his grace.

Result of Illusion

चिच्छायाऽऽवेशतो बुद्धौ भानं धीस्तु द्विधा स्थिता ।

एकाहंकृतिरन्या स्यात् अन्तःकरणरूपिणी ॥ ६ ॥

Citchāyā'veśato buddhau bhānaṃ dhīstu dvidhā sthitā |

Ekāhañkrutiranya syat antaḥkaraṇarūpiṇi || 6 ||

Meaning: Intellect (Buddhi, बुद्धि) appears to be sentient due to the reflected light of Ātman. Intellect is of two kinds - One is the ego (Ahaṅkāra, अहंकार) while the other is the mind (Antaḥkaraṇa, अंतःकरण).

Light permeates completely in a diamond, since it is clear and transparent, but not in a stone. Likewise, intellect (Buddhi) is clean and clear, since it is made up of the fire element and Sattva Guṇa. It is made up of the 'five great elements' in their pure form (Apañchīkṛta Pañcamahābhūtas, अपंचीकृत पंचमहाभूते). As a result, the divine light of Ātman reflects in the intellect, and the reflection is called as **Cidābhāsa** (चिदाभास). Intellect appears to be sentient on account of the reflection of Pure Consciousness in it. Intellect pervades the whole body, so the gross body appears to be sentient as well. The efficiency of the intellect (remembering, decision making) may vary from person to person, but the reflection of Consciousness is the same across all intellects.

The mind (Manas, मन), intellect (Buddhi, बुद्धि), memory (Citta, चित्त) and ego (Ahaṅkāra, अहंकार) together form Antaḥkaraṇa (अंतःकरण). So technically, the ego is a part of Antaḥkaraṇa. However, in this verse, the ego and the Antaḥkaraṇa are categorized separately. The reason for this separation is that the mind, the intellect and the Citta work only with the support of the ego. E.g. 'I desire', 'my decision' and 'I concentrate' are examples of how the mind, the intellect and the Citta work in conjunction with the ego respectively.

Desires by the mind, decision by the intellect and concentration by the Citta do not have an isolated presence. These mental states always exist in conjunction with 'I' or the ego. Be it the mind, the intellect or the Citta, ego is an integral part of their functioning. In other words, the ego takes charge of these three faculties. The illusion that 'I am the mind', 'I am the intellect', 'I am the Citta' are examples of superimposition of the ego on the three faculties of Antaḥkaraṇa. 'I am great', 'I am beautiful', 'I am ugly', 'I am rich' are the examples of superimposition of the ego on the body and circumstances. This superimposed (Adhyasta, अध्यस्त) ego is manifestation of the constant instinct of existence based on the principle of Sat (eternal Pure Existence). Eradication of this superimposed ego should be the main goal of any spiritual practice. Superimposition (Adhyasta) does not have an autonomous existence without its substratum (Adhiṣṭhāna, अधिष्ठान). So superimposed ego has no separate existence without the substratum of Ātman.

Identification of the Ego and Reflected Consciousness

छायाहंकारयोरैक्यं तप्तायः पिंडवन्मतम् ।
तदहंकारतादात्म्यात् देहश्चैतनतामगात् ॥ ७ ॥

Chāyāhañkārayoraikyaṃ taptāyaḥ piñḍavanmatam /
Tadahañkāratādātmyāt dehaścaitanatāmagāt // 7 //

Meaning: In a heated iron ball, fire and the iron ball appear to be identified with each other. Likewise, the ego and Reflected Consciousness (Cidābhāsa, चिदाभास) appear identified with each other. The insentient (जड़, Jaḍa) body appears to be sentient (चेतन, Cetan) as a result of its identification with the ego that is already unified with the Reflected Consciousness.

When an iron ball is kept in fire, it gradually becomes red in color. Fire is identified with the iron ball (Tādātmya Saṃbandha, तादात्म्य संबंध). As a result, redness of iron is identified with the iron ball and roundness of the ball is identified with the fire. This is also called as Anyonyādhyāsa (अन्योन्याध्यास).

Similarly, the Reflected Consciousness identifies itself with the ego. They cannot be separated from each other. As a result, insentient ego appears to be sentient, while sentient Reflected Consciousness appears to be insentient. e.g.: I am tall, I am rich, and I am brilliant etc. are the manifestations of the ego, but they wrongly appear to be manifestations of the Reflected Consciousness. Ātman is the illuminator while Reflected Consciousness is illumined by Ātman. However, both of them are comprehended at the same time. Pure Consciousness is naturally present wherever there is Reflected Consciousness. Pure Consciousness is Ātman (Dṛk), Reflected Consciousness is the perceiver (Draṣṭā), and the world is perceivable (Dṛśya).

Three Types of Identification of the Ego

अहंकारस्य तादात्म्यं चिच्छायादेहसाक्षिभिः ।

सहजं कर्मजं भ्रान्तिजन्यं च त्रिविधं क्रमात् ॥ ८ ॥

Ahaṅkārasya tādātmyaṃ cichāyadehasākṣībhih |
Sahajaṃ karmajaṃ bhrāntijanyan cha trividhaṃ kramāt || 8 ||

Meaning: The identification of the ego with the Reflected Consciousness (Cidābhāsa) is named as 'natural' (Sahaja Tādātmya), identification of the ego with the body is attributed to 'past Karma' (Karmaja Tādātmya), and identification of the ego with the Witness (Sākṣī) is termed as 'illusory' (Bhramaja Tādātmya).

Natural (Sahaja Tādātmya, सहज तादात्म्य) - The mind is the medium of reflecting Pure Consciousness. So, whenever the mind is present (i.e. it is awake), it naturally has Reflected Consciousness in it. The ego that is felt in the very first moment of waking up is naturally identified with the Reflected Consciousness. As soon as eyes open and see an object, the mind (**Vṛttī**, वृत्ती) takes form of that object, hence the object is known. This process is called as **Vṛttījñyana** (वृत्तिज्ञान). The natural identification between the ego (Ahaṅkāra, अहंकार) and Reflected Consciousness results in the creation of the knower or perceiver (Jīva). All knowledge in everyday life is based on this identification.

Past Karma (Karmaja Tādātmya, कर्मज तादात्म्य) - There are three kinds of actions associated with human life -

- Sañciṭa Karma (संचित कर्म): Accumulated actions of a Jīva (embodied soul) from all past human births. Jīva has to bear results of all accumulated actions (good or bad). After Self-realization, these accumulated actions are completely eradicated, which otherwise need to be endured by Jīva.
- Prārabdha Karma (प्रारब्ध कर्म): Fructescent actions from Sañciṭa Karma, on account of which Jīva gets his body in the current birth. The body lasts so long as these actions continue to produce their results.

- Kriyamāṇa Karma (क्रियमाण कर्म): Fresh new actions performed by Jīva. If new actions are done with 'I am the doer' mindset and in a selfish manner, they get added to the Sañciṭa of that Jīva.

Birth of a Jīva in a particular body is always dictated by his past actions. The ego identifies itself with a specific body to perform fresh new actions. The pleasures of reading, climbing mountains, eating etc. are enjoyed by the ego only with the help of a body as a medium. The gender-based differences pertain to body, but they appear to be pertaining to the ego (I am man, I am woman etc.). Everyday life cannot proceed without considering these differences.

From the spiritual perspective, the Pure Consciousness (Dṛk / the real Self) does not have a gender. Gross body is made up of 3 Guṇas and 5 Great elements (Aṣṭadhā Prakṛtī, अष्टधा प्रकृती), so it is insentient (Jaḍa, जड) in nature. The identification with Reflected Consciousness imparts the appearance of sentience to body.

Illusory (Bhramaja Tādātmya, भ्रमज तादात्म्य) – Pure Consciousness or Ātman or the Witness (Sākṣī / Kutastha) is sentient (Cetan, चेतन), changeless and Pure Bliss in itself. The ego is insentient, changeable and experiencer of both joys and sorrow. The identification of the ego with the Pure Consciousness is a result of delusion or error (Bhrānti, भ्रांती). It does not exist for real. The ego undergoes modifications or changes. E.g. feelings of anger, jealousy, greed, hatred, pride, cravings etc. Pure Consciousness, which is the real Self, is changeless but due to the process of false superimposition (Adhyāsa, अध्यास), it is delusively perceived as 'I am greedy' or 'I am jealous' etc. The ego gets divided (Pariccheda, परिच्छेद). E.g. the difference such as 'I am tall or short' arises on account of body, 'I am smart or dumb' arises on account of the intellect (Buddhi), 'I am rich or poor' arises on account of the circumstances. Ātman is the only one eternal Ultimate Truth (Satya, सत्य). So, it cannot be divided in this manner. The ego experiences suffering, misery, anguish, worry or repentance. Ātman, which is Pure Bliss, does not ever suffer in any manner.

Eradication of the Three Identifications

संबन्धिनोस्सतोर्नास्ति निवृत्तिस्सहजस्य तु ।
कर्मक्षयात् प्रबोधाच्च निवर्तेते क्रमादुभे ॥ ९ ॥

Saṃbandhinosstornāsti nivṛttissahajasya tu |
Karmakshayāt prabodhācca nivartete kramādubhe || 9 ||

Meaning: The natural identification of the ego with the Reflected Consciousness (Cidābhāsa) does not end. The identification of the ego with body is eradicated after wearing out of the results of actions (Karmakshaya,

कर्मक्षय). The deceptive identification of the ego with the Witness (Sākṣī) disappears after Self-realization.

Even after enlightenment, the natural identification of the ego with the Reflected Consciousness does not end. It is not even necessary for it to come to an end. No separate spiritual practice is needed to eradicate it. Day-to-day activities cannot be conducted without this identification. It naturally stays intact even in the Self-realized person. This identification is needed to sustain life as dictated by the destiny (Prārabdha Karma, प्रारब्ध कर्म). After enlightenment, this identification has very little value or importance. One should not be deluded by the thought that spiritual practice has not reached culmination due to the presence of this natural identification.

The identification of the ego with a particular body is a result of the Prārabdha Karma of that Jīva (embodied soul). The effects of this identification are seen so long as Prārabdha continues to produce its effects. Physical body comes to an end as a result of complete wearing out of the result of Prārabdha. The identification of the ego with a body automatically ends with the death of that body.

Bhagvad-Gītā says -

ज्ञानाग्निः सर्व कर्माणि भस्मसात् कुरुते तथा ।

Jñyānāgniḥ sarva karmāṇi bhasmasāt kurute tathā | (4-37).

- 'After the ultimate Knowledge of Brahman, all accumulated actions (Sañciṭa) from past births are turned into ashes. It means they stop being fruitive and do not produce any result.'

Śruti says -

स विद्वान्पुण्यपापे विधूय परमसाम्यमुपैति । (Muṇḍaka Up. 3.1.3)

Sa vidvān puṇyapāpe vidhūya paramasāmyamupaiti |

- 'A Self-realized sage performs day-to-day actions (Kriyamāṇa Karma) without any expectations. So, they do not produce any fruits or results. They are not binding for him. Prārabdha Karma comes to an end after fully living through its effects.'

The identification of the ego with the Witness (Ātman) is a result of error or delusion (bhrānti). It ends only after attainment of the highest Knowledge of Ātman i.e. Self-realization. Knowledge of Ātman destroys delusion and ignorance. Ego dissolves in Ātman after Self-realization, so it can no longer identify with the Witness (Sākṣī). The identification of the ego with the Witness, thus comes to an end.

Analysis of the Three States of Jīva

अहंकारलये सुप्तौ भवेद्देहोऽप्यचेतनः ।
अहंकारविकासार्धः स्वप्नः सर्वस्तु जागरः ॥ १० ॥

Ahaṅkāralaye suptāu bhaveddeho'pyacetanaḥ |

Ahaṅkāravikāsārdhaḥ svapnaḥ sarvastu jāgaraḥ || 10 ||

Meaning: The ego dissolves in the state of deep-sleep. As a result of that, the body becomes unconscious. In the dream state, the ego is half awake or partially manifested. In the state of waking, the ego is fully manifested.

Dṛk (Ātman) transcends the three states of waking, dream and deep-sleep. These three states are mutually exclusive (Vyatireka, व्यतिरेक). A person is neither awake nor in deep-sleep while he is dreaming. A person is neither awake nor dreaming during deep-sleep. A person is neither dreaming nor in deep-sleep when he is awake. But Ātman (Pure Consciousness) pervades all these three states yet stays fully detached from them. Ātman is stable, constant and unchanging, while the three states begin, sustain and end in a cyclic manner. They get subtly converted into each other.

In the state of deep-sleep, the ego dissolves in causal body (Kāraṇa deha, कारण देह). It gets separated from the gross body for the duration of deep-sleep. As a result, the gross body becomes heavy while sleeping. Bṛihadāraṇyaka Upaniṣad says -

अत्र पिता अपिता भवति । स्तेनो अस्तेनो भवति ॥ (4.3.22)

Atra pitā apitā bhavati | Steno asteno bhavati ||

- 'A person who is in deep-sleep forgets whether he is a father or a thief etc.'

In the state of waking, the ego carries the weight of the body, since it identifies with the body, so the body does not feel heavy. In the dream state, the ego is partially manifested. It identifies itself with the subtle body (Sūkṣma deha, सूक्ष्म देह). So, the person (who is dreaming) is unable to discriminate between the reality and the dream. One may see a lake or an elephant, but it is only the mind that takes the form of a lake or an elephant while dreaming. Any object or event seen in the dream does not exist for real. After waking up, the person says, 'I saw a dream', since the ego was partially present at that time. The mind understands that the entire dream sequence was just an illusion.

The ego is fully manifested in the waking state. It identifies with the gross body and subtle body. As a result, a person wakes up in his entirety. All objects are perceived as different entities by him. He knows and understands these objects. All memories are awakened. However, it is extremely difficult to comprehend the fact that the waking state is as illusory (Mithyā, मिथ्या) as the states of dream and deep-sleep. Some people speak or walk while sleeping. Some people get scared while dreaming and wake up suddenly. They feel relieved that they have come out of bad dream. Some dreams get realized in the waking state. But all these incidents are as illusory as actual dream sequences. The Vedānta doctrine acts as a bulldozer, which flattens everything that comes its way, including the sense of reality in the waking state.

Secret Behind the Dream and the Waking State

अन्तःकरणवृत्तिश्च चितिच्छायैक्यमागता ।

वासना कल्पयेत् स्वप्ने बोधेऽक्षैर्विषयान् बहिः ॥ ११ ॥

Antaḥkaraṇavṛttiśca citicchāyaikyamāgatā /

Vāsanā kalpayet svapne bodhe'kṣairviṣayān bahiḥ // 11 //

Meaning: The mind (Antaḥkaraṇa, अंतःकरण) identifies itself with the Reflected Consciousness (Cidābhāsa, चिदाभास) and imagines various ideas in the dream. The same mind takes help of the sense organs in the waking state and imagines various objects external to itself.

Humans carry imprints of varied experiences from many past births. As a result, dreams are not necessarily related to events in current life. Dreams are not coherent since they have a mixture of many experiences. E.g. the stacks of neatly organized notes in a bank are seen to be present in a house in a dream. A person travelling in an airplane might be seen cycling the very next moment.

Everyday stress and tensions in the waking state get manifested in dreams as well. These are nothing but ideas of the mind and modifications in the state of the mind.

Māṇḍūkya Kārika says -

यथा स्वप्ने द्वयाभासं स्पन्दते मायया मनः ।

तथा जाग्रद्द्वयाभासं स्पन्दते मायया मनः ॥ (३-२९)

मनोदृश्यमिदं द्वैतं यत्किंचित्सचराचरम् ।

मनसो ह्यमनीभावे द्वैतं नैवोपलभ्यते ॥ (३-३१)

Yathā svapne dvayābhāsaṃ spandate Māyayā manaḥ |

Tathā jāgraddvayābhāsaṃ spandate Māyāya manaḥ || (3-29)

Manodṛśyamidaṃ dvaitaṃ yatkincitsacarācaraṃ |

Manaso hyamanībhāve dvaitaṃ naivopalabhyate || (3-31)

- 'Due to the influence of Māyā, there is an illusory perception of duality in dreams. Likewise, what we see in the waking state is an illusory picture of duality as well. All sentient and insentient objects in the world are nothing but modifications in the mind. These objects and the perceived duality cease to exist when the mind is dissolved in the process of Self-realization i.e. when it becomes completely clear, quiet and devoid of thoughts.'

Formation of the Subtle Body

मनोऽहंकृत्युपादानं लिंगमेकं जडात्मकम् ।

अवस्थात्रयमन्वेति जायते म्रियते तथा ॥ १२ ॥

Mano'haṅkrutyupādānaṃ liṅgamekaṃ jaḍātmakam |

Avasthātrayamanveti jāyate mriyate tathā || 12 ||

Meaning: The ego and the mind come together to become material cause (Upādān Kāraṇa) of the subtle body (Sūkṣma deha). The subtle body is insentient (Jaḍa, जड) in nature. It has the three states of waking, dream and deep-sleep. It goes through the cycle of birth, life and death. The subtle body is also known as Liṅga Deha (लिंग देह).

After death, the subtle body with mental imprints of the past births (Vāsanā, वासना) enters the next new body. Subtle body, gross body and causal body are all insentient in nature. The perception of sentience (Caitanya, चैतन्य) in a body is due to Reflected Consciousness (Cidābhāsa, चिदाभास) in it. Insentient body cannot die. Pure Consciousness is sentient, and it cannot die as well. So, the idea of death should not bring in misery or unhappiness.

The insentient subtle body constantly goes through the cycle of birth, life and death. Ātman (Dṛk or Pure Consciousness) is birthless, ageless and deathless (Aja-अज, Ajara-अजर, Amara-अमर). Both the subtle body and Ātman are eternal in their own ways. Subtle body is perceived to be eternal as it constantly undergoes the life-death cycle due to the impact of Māyā. Pure Consciousness is sentient and eternal.

So far, we have analyzed birth and death of body on an individual level. Next verses explain the creation of all objects on universal level. All objects are insentient. So why are they perceived to be real and sentient?

The Powers of Māyā

शक्ति द्वयं ही मायाया विक्षेपावृत्तिरूपकम् ।
विक्षेपशक्तिर्लिंगादि ब्रह्मांडान्तं जगत् सृजेत् ॥ १३ ॥

Śakti dvayaṃ hi Māyāya vikeshpāvṛttirūpakam |
Vikṣepaśaktirliṅgādi Brahmāndāntaṃ jagat sṛjet || 13 ||

Meaning: Māyā undeniably has two powers, which are 'projecting' (Vikṣepa, विक्षेप) and 'veiling' (Āvaraṇa, आवरण). The perceiver and every perceived object (the entire Universe) gets created by the projection power of Māyā.

Māyā is that, which has only perceptual existence. It does not exist for real, but it appears to be real. Five sense organs, five action organs and the five great elements (Pañca-Mahābhūta) are all different aspects of Māyā.

These aspects are meant only to comprehend and logically analyze the differences amongst all objects. Māyā itself has no real existence, so it cannot be divided into different aspects. These aspects are falsely attributed on Māyā (Adhyāropa, अध्यारोप). Māyā is **Aghaṭita-ghaṭanā-paṭiyasī** (अघटित-घटना-पटियसी), which means it is adept at showing creations and incidences that are totally inconceivable. All activities and changes in the world occur due to this Aghatita-ghatnā-patiyasi attribute of Māyā.

A verse in Gītā says -

अज्ञानेनावृतं ज्ञानं । (5.15)

Ajñānenāvṛtaṃ Jñānaṃ /

- 'Māyā puts a veil on Pure Knowledge (Ātman).'

Since Māyā performs the action of veiling, it cannot be considered as completely non-existent. St. Madhusudan Saraswati says that it needs to be given imaginary existence for the same reason.

Māyā is named differently according to six imaginary actions it performs. Various names for Māyā are -

Māyā (माया) - The powers of Māyā are inconceivable, but they can be made inconsequential after enlightenment. Hence it is named as Māyā.

Avidyā (अविद्या) - Māyā disappears and becomes inconsequential after Brahma-Vidya i.e. after Pure Knowledge of Brahman is realized, hence called as Avidyā.

Ajñāna (अज्ञान) - Ajñāna (ignorance) does not mean lack of Jñāna or knowledge. Ajñāna means that, which prevents knowledge of Ātman or the real Self. Ignorance is the main reason behind illusion (Bhrama, भ्रम). Māyā covers Brahman with a veil, which prevents the knowledge of the Self. It maintains a state of ignorance about the true nature of the Self, hence called as Ajñāna. It can be removed only with the grace of Sadguru.

Prakṛti (प्रकृति) - The Universe and all entities are essentially made up of the three Guṇās (qualities of material nature i.e. Sattva, Rajas and Tamas). The creation of the Universe takes place primarily from Tamas Guṇā (ignorance). When Māyā becomes predominantly Tāmasi in nature in order to create the cosmos, it is called as prakruti.

Śakti (शक्ति) - Śakti means power. Power does not have autonomous existence. Any power needs a person/entity to manifest itself. Māyā exists and sustains due to Pure Consciousness (Caitanya, चैतन्य). It manifests its powers in various forms with Caitanya as its only anchor. Hence, called as Śakti.

Pradhāna or Avyakta (प्रधान, अव्यक्त) - After the end of cosmos (Pralaya, प्रलय), when the Universe (Brahmaṇḍa, ब्रह्मांड) ceases to exist, all sentient and insentient entities stay in the seed form (Bīja, बीज) in the principle named Pradhāna.

The veiling power of Māyā covers and hides Brahman, which is the Eternal Truth (Satya, सत्य). Due to the projection power of Māyā, the Universe is deceptively seen in the place of Brahman. E.g. during dusk time, a rope gets covered and hidden due to dim light, and a snake is deceptively seen in its place. The rope (as if) gets covered by the snake and becomes invisible. It cannot be known in its original form. Similarly, Brahman gets deceptively covered by the visible world due to the veiling power of Māyā. The world is delusively created due to the projection power of Māyā. The world is a delusion, just like the snake that is delusively seen on the rope. Knowledge of Brahman cannot be attained unless these two powers of Māyā are rendered ineffective.

St. Sureśvarācārya says that the illusion caused by Māyā cannot possibly exist for real.

नाहं न च ममात्मत्वात्सर्वदानाऽत्मवर्जितः ।

भानाविव तमोऽध्यासोऽपह्नवश्च तथा मयि ॥ (Naishk. Siddhi 2.117)

Nāhaṃ na ca mamātmatvātsarvadānā'tmavarjitaḥ /

Bhānāviva tamo'dhyāsao'pahnavaśca tathā mayi //

- 'The feelings of ego and mineness cannot be falsely superimposed (Adhyasta, अध्यस्त) on the real Self i.e. Ātman. It is not possible to eradicate darkness when the Sun is present. Likewise, it is not possible to remove the false superimposition of ego and mineness in the eternal presence of Ātman.'

But even then -

तथाऽप्याभाति कोऽप्येषविचाराभावजीवनः ।

अवश्यायश्चिदाकाशे विचारार्कोदयावधिः ॥ (Advaita Makarand 17)

Tathāpyā'bhāti kopye'ṣavicārābhāvajivanaḥ /

Avaśyāyaścidākāśe vicārārkodayāvadhiḥ //

St. Laxmidhara says that the ignorance (Ajñāna) about the real Self is due to the lack of thinking and discrimination (Vivēka, विवेक) between real and non-real aspects of life. Ignorance has delusive and perceptual existence. When the Sun of Pure Knowledge of Bṛahman rises, the ignorance gets eradicated.

The power of projection of Māyā gets assistance from the mind. Śri Ramaṇa Maharśi says that every duality and triad (e.g. knower, knowable and knowledge) is supported by the substratum of Brahman. All dualities and triads need to be gradually discarded in the process of realizing Brahman. Self-realization takes place once the triad is dissolved i.e. the knower becomes one with the knowable.

Māṇḍūkya Kārika says -

मायामात्रं इदं द्वैतं अद्वैतं परमार्थतः । (1.17)

Māyāmātraṃ idaṃ dvaitaṃ advaitaṃ Paramārthataḥ /

- 'Dvaita (duality) is incorrectly perceived only due to the presence of the illusory mind. In reality, only Advaita (non-duality) exists.'

Māṇḍūkya Kārika has taken a standpoint that -

प्रपंचो यदि विद्येत निवर्तेत न संशयः । (1.17)

Prapañcho yadi vidyeta nivarteta na sañśayaḥ /

-'If the world had existed for real, it would have been possible to eradicate it. (However, since it cannot be discarded or eradicated, it does not have real existence.)'

The illusion of the dual world (Dṛśya) takes place on the substratum of Ātman (Dṛk).

The Nature of Creation

सृष्टिर्नाम ब्रह्मरूपे सच्चिदानन्दवस्तुनि ।

अब्धौ फेनादिवत्सर्वनामरुपप्रसारणा ॥ १४ ॥

Sruṣtirnāma Brahmarūpe Saccidānandavastuni |

Abdhau phenādivatsarvanāmarūpaprasāraṇā || 14 ||

Meaning: Brahman is Sat, Cit, Ānanda i.e. (Pure) Existence, Consciousness, Bliss. Manifestation of various names and forms is delusively seen on the substratum of Brahman, just like ripples, waves, drops and foam are seen in the ocean.

There is a verse in Upaniṣad, which describes the creation of sentient and insentient entities -

एकोऽहम् बहुस्याम् । *Eko'ham bahusyām |*

- '(Brahman thinks) I am One and I (would like to) manifest in many forms.'

The manifold Universe was created from this instinctive thought of Brahman per the theory of False Attribution (Adhyāropa, अध्यारोप). Every manifested entity in the world is perceivable. Entities which can be 'seen' are not the only ones that are termed as 'perceivable'. Anything that is known, understood, experimented, proved, experienced in dreams, contemplated or discerned is termed as 'perceivable' (Dṛśya, दृश्य).

A single entity may have many names or forms. E.g. a watch may have many forms (different shapes, metallic or plastic body etc.) and it is known by different names in different languages. Every form has its own elements. E.g. a brick that gets used in construction has soil particles as its elements. Soil is a form of the Earth element (Pṛthvī Mahabhūta, पृथ्वी महाभूत), which is preceded by the water, the fire, the wind, the sky element and Ātman. There is enormous variety in all names and forms, but all of them delusively appear and disappear in Brahman. Only Ātman is Dṛk, while everything else is Dṛśya i.e. seen or perceived.

The Power of Veiling

अन्तर्दृग्दृश्ययोर्भेदं बहिश्च ब्रह्मसर्गयोः ।
आवृणोत्यपराशक्तिः सा संसारस्य कारणम् ॥ १५ ॥

Antardṛgdṛśyaorbhedam bahiśca Brahmasargayoḥ |
Avṛṇotyaparāśaktiḥ sā sañsārasya kāraṇam || 15 ||

Meaning: The veiling power of Māyā conceals the distinction between the Witness (Dṛk) and the perceived objects, which are cognized inside (the body). It also conceals the distinction between Brahman and the world, which is cognized outside (the body). This veiling power is the cause of the phenomenal Universe.

Ātman is considered to be present inside the perceiver's body and Brahman is considered to be present outside the body for the context of this verse.

The veiling power of Māyā works in two ways. Internally, the Witness is separate from the objects that it witnesses. E.g. the Witness is separate from the mind. Māyā creates an internal veil due to which the distinction between the Witness and objects is not seen. As a result, the Witness appears to have identified itself with the body, mind, sense organs etc. Due to this identification, the Witness thinks 'I am body' 'I am enjoyer' etc. and perceives himself to be separate from the all-pervasive Brahman.

Externally, Māyā veils the distinction between Brahman and the world. Brahman is non-dual, while the visible world is full of duality and variations. The appearance of multiplicity in the world is due to the external veil of Māyā, which delusively shows creation and destruction of many objects on the substratum of Brahman.

Brahman, which is present inside the body may be called as Ātman. Ātman, which is present outside the body may be called as Brahman. As soon as the limiting adjunct (Upādhi) of the body is discarded in thoughts, both Ātman and Brahman are One.

When the Sun is covered by the dense fog, it cannot be seen. But the fog itself is seen in the light of the Sun. Similarly, the perceiver cannot clearly discern the reality due to the veil of Māyā. He gets deceived into thinking that, 'the world exists for real, Ātman does not exist, I am body and the world is full of many varied entities'. Only a chosen few seekers (based on past karma) get to even hear or read that the manifold appearance of the Universe is due to the veiling power of Māyā. An exceptional seeker contemplates and assimilates this fact. Realization that 'I am Ātman' paves the way for blissful life. This process involves the grace of scriptures, Sadguru, Īśvara and Ātman. The veil of Māyā can be discerned only in the light of Ātman, just like the fog that covers the Sun, gets seen only in the sunlight.

The process of creation, sustenance and destruction continues both inside and outside the body. At some point, everything comes to an end. One changeless, constant principle exists in this ever-changing Universe. That principle is named Ātman or Brahman. It is the real nature of 'I'. Ātman is birth-less and end-less (Aja-अज, Amara-अमर) and 'I am that Ātman'. Logically witnessing all events inside and outside body is an effective form of spiritual practice.

Internal Veil Hides the Distinction between the Witness and the Mind (Jīva)

साक्षिणः पुरतो भातं लिंगं देहेन संयुतम् ।
चितिच्छायासमावेशात् जीवः स्याद् व्यावहारिकः ॥ १६ ॥

Sākṣīṇaḥ purato bhātaṃ liṅgaṃ dehen sanyutam |
Citicchāyāsamāveśāt jivaḥ syad vyāvahārikaḥ || 16 ||

Meaning: The Witness (Pure Consciousness) appears as if it is manifested (in gross body), when it is reflected in the subtle body. The embodied self (Jīva) gets created due to the Reflected Consciousness in the subtle body.

The mind (Antaḥkaraṇa, अंतःकरण) is a part of the subtle body. Pure Consciousness is the Witness, which gets reflected in the mind. Due to the presence of this Reflected Consciousness, the mind starts thinking that all activities performed by the gross body are performed by itself. The mind is insentient. However, it considers itself to be sentient due to the presence of Reflected Consciousness. This is termed as Sansargādhyāsa (संसर्गाध्यास). All worldly activities are conducted by the union of the mind and Reflected Consciousness. Together they are called as **Jīva** (embodied or individual self).

In reality, only Pure Consciousness is complete and all-pervasive. But due to close association with the mind, it considers itself as incomplete and limited. It makes a futile attempt to lead a complete, meaningful, perpetual and blissful life with the help of gross body. This delusion of association between Reflected Consciousness and the gross body ends only when the veiling power of Māyā becomes ineffective.

The Result of Disappearance of the Internal Veil of Māyā

अस्य जीवत्वमारोपात् साक्षिण्यप्यवभासते ।
आवृतौ तु विनष्टायां भेदे भातेऽपयाति तत् ॥ १७ ॥

Asya jīvātvamāropāt sākṣīṇyapyavabhāsate |
Āvṛtau tu vinaṣṭāyāṃ bheḍe bhāte'payāti tat || 17 ||

Meaning: The Witness (Pure Consciousness) appears as if it is the embodied self (Jīva) due to false superimposition (Adhyāsa, अध्यास). The distinction between them becomes clear when the veiling power becomes ineffective. Consequently, the idea of being a separate embodied self (Jīva) disappears.

A person sitting on a tree-trunk on the shore of a river sees his reflection in the river water. The foam, ripples and garbage in the water appear to be superimposed on the reflection. But the person does not strive to remove them. He knows that foam and garbage are superimposed on his reflection, and not on himself. Similarly, the characteristics of the Reflected Consciousness should not be superimposed on Ātman i.e. Pure Consciousness.

Jīva has a body, mind and intellect (with Reflected Consciousness). The body of a particular Jīva may be fat or thin, and his intellect may be brilliant or immature. Jīva may be living a rich or poor life. The Reflected Consciousness considers all of these characteristics (fat, thin, intelligent, rich, and poor) to be its own. Due to false superimposition, the Witness (Ātman) appears as if it is Jīva, who has assumed the characteristics of body, mind etc. to be its own.

The real I or Self is Ātman, which has no form, body, mind or intellect. It transcends all perceivable entities in the world. The person sitting on the branch focuses on himself and ignores the garbage on his reflection in the water. He does not wait for the reflection to become stable or clear. Similarly, even if the Reflected Consciousness is associated with many characteristics, they should not be falsely superimposed on Ātman, which is the real Self.

External Veil Hides the Distinction between Brahman and the World

तथा सर्ग-ब्रह्मणोश्च भेदमावृत्य तिष्ठति ।

या शक्तिस्तद्वशाद्ब्रह्म विकृतत्वेन भासते ॥ १८ ॥

Tathā sarga brahmaṇośca bhedamāvṛtya tiśthati |

Yā śaktistadvaśādbrahma vikṛtatvena bhāsate || 18 ||

Meaning: The veiling power of Māyā conceals the distinction between Brahman and the visible world. As a result of that power, Brahman appears in a distorted form, endowed with the attributes of the world.

Brahman and the world share the illuminator-illumined relationship (Prakāśaka-Prakāśya, प्रकाशक-प्रकाश्य). Brahman is the illuminator and sentient. The world is illumined and insentient. The veiling power of Māyā conceals the distinction between Brahman and the world and does not let it be explicitly known.

Māyā is Aghaṭita-ghaṭanā-paṭiyasī (अघटित-घटना-पटीयसी), which means it is adept at showing creations and incidences that are totally inconceivable. Due to this attribute of Māyā, the distinction between Brahman and the world becomes imperceptible. The world appears to be sentient, while Brahman (Ātman) appears to be insentient. The body of the perceiver appears to be sentient, while Ātman appears to be mortal (E.g. I am going to die). Brahman, which is Sat (eternal), becomes incomprehensible. Brahman undergoes Vivarta i.e. imaginary change. Vivarta is the change, where the perceived object is different from its substratum both visually and in essence. As a result of Vivarta, Brahman gets completely hidden. There is an illusory appearance of the world on the substratum of Brahman. Many names and forms conceal Brahman. Ādi Śaṅkarācārya says in Bṛihadāraṇyak Bhāśya -

अध्यारोपितनामरूपकर्मद्वारेण ब्रह्म निर्दिश्यते ।

Adhyāropita nāma rūpa karma dwāreṇa brahma nirdiśyate /

- 'We can infer Brahman is present wherever a name or a form or an activity is seen. Any name, form and activity point to Brahman.'

The Result of Disappearance of the External Veil of Māyā

अत्राप्यावृत्तिनाशेन विभाति ब्रह्म-सर्गयोः ।
भेदस्तयोर्विकारः स्यात् सर्गे न ब्रह्मणि क्वचित् ॥ १९ ॥

Atrāpyāvṛttināśen vibhāti Brahma-sargayoḥ /
Bhedāstāyorvikaraḥ syāt sarge na Brahmaṇi kvacit // *19* //

Meaning: Here as well (like verse 17), the distinction between Brahman and the world becomes clear when the veiling power of Māyā disappears. Therefore, it can be understood that the attributes of creation, destruction, change etc. are present in the world, but never in Brahman itself.

As mentioned in verse 17, in the case of an individual self, the distinction between Jīva and Ātman becomes clear when the internal veiling power becomes ineffective. Here, verse 19 talks about how the distinction between Brahman and the world becomes clear when the external veil of Māyā becomes ineffective.

The mind takes the form of an object when it perceives the object. If the object is changed, the changes are reflected in the mind i.e. the mind gets modified. However, behind every modification or change, there is one changeless principle. The concept of speed is relative to the stationary objects. The speed of the train is relative to the immobile rail tracks. The thought that 'this is gold' remains the same, even if gold is modified and split into various ornaments. Similarly, Dṛk i.e. the substratum on which the mind works, is stable and constant in nature; even if the mind is constantly changing, wavering and unstable. The process of birth and death takes place in a cyclic manner. However, there is one changeless, constant principle of Dṛk (Pure Consciousness) behind the cycle.

On the personal level, Ātman (Dṛk) is beginning-less, ageless and endless (Aja-अज, Ajara-अजर and Amara-अमर). On the Universal level, Brahman does not get created, sustained or destroyed. Piṇḍa and Brahmāṇḍa (individual self and Universal self) are both destructible and hence they fall in the same category. Ātman and Brahman are both eternal, hence One in essence.

Five Parts of the Visible World (Dṛśya)

अस्ति भाति प्रियं रूपं नाम चेत्यंशपंचकम् ।
आद्यत्रयं ब्रह्मरूपं जगद्रूपं ततो द्वयम् ॥ २० ॥

Asti bhāti priyaṃ rūpaṃ nāma cetyaṇśapañcakam |
Ādyatrayaṃ Brahmarūpaṃ jagadrūpaṃ tato dvayam || 20 ||

Meaning: Every perceivable object has five attributes - existence, cognizance, likeability, name and form. The first three are related to Dṛk i.e. Brahman. The last two belong to the world.

- **Empirical reality** (Vyāvahārika Sattā, व्यावहारिक सत्ता)
  - The world with name and forms
- **Divine reality** (Īśvarī Sattā, ईश्वरी सत्ता)
  - Existence (Asti, अस्ति)
  - Cognizance (Bhāti, भाति)
  - Likeability (Priya, प्रिय)
- **Absolute reality** (Pārmārthika Sattā, पारमार्थिक सत्ता)
  - Sat, Cit, Ānanda

Śruti explains the creation of the Universe in two different ways -

1. Sequentially: Ātman - Māyā - Three Guṇas - Five Great Elements - All visible objects
2. Simultaneously: The entire Universe was instantly created with all its entities at the same time

Irrespective of how or when the Universe was created, it is illusory (Mithyā, मिथ्या) in nature. One should not be attached to it. This is the real crux of the ideal human life.

When an object with a name and form is seen, one may like it, dislike it or be neutral towards it. Liking leads to happiness, disliking leads to distress, while neutrality leads to the lack of reaction. Names and forms may be many, but the three factors of existence, cognizance, likeability (Asti, Bhāti, Priya) are common amongst all objects. All objects 'exist', they can be 'cognized' and they have a 'likeability quotient'. Diseases or harmful animals are 'liked' when they 'do not exist'. Hence, they too are likeable. Existence and cognizance are the same for all objects. These three attributes are more long-lasting than the individual objects. Thousands of names and forms may get destructed, but the 'principle of existence' persists due to the remaining names and forms. This existence lasts until the end of the Universe. Even after the end of the Cosmos (Pralaya, प्रलय), Pure Existence i.e. Sat (Brahman) still exists. Same is the case with cognizance and likeability. Cognizance comes from Pure Knowledge and likeability comes from Pure Bliss of Brahman. Brahman is constant, beginning-less, endless, the most primitive and eternally existent.

If a mango is peeled and juiced, its seed still carries the unique taste and aroma of the mango. Similarly, there is a little taste of Sat-Cit-Ānanda in the existence, cognizance, and likeability characteristics of the world. The existence of insentient entities in the world is the 'taste of Sat'. All faculties of knowledge and happiness are the 'tastes of Cit and Ānanda' of Brahman. The entire world survives on the little taste of Brahman. Taittiriya Śruti says -

रसं ह्येवायं लब्ध्वाऽनंदी भवति

Rasaṃ hyevāyaṃ labdhvā ānandi bhavati (2-7)

- 'The nectar of this Ātman gives (everyone) Supreme Bliss.'

One can imagine the taste of the original mango just by tasting its seed. Similarly, one should reflect on the Bliss of Ātman just by looking at its manifestations in everyday life.

Brahman is All-Pervasive

खंवाय्वग्निजलोर्वीषु देवतिर्यंनरादिषु ।
अभिन्नास्सच्चिदानन्दाः भिद्येते रूपनामनी ॥ २१ ॥

Khaṃvāyavagnijalorvīṣu devatiryaññarādiṣu |

Abhinnassaccidānandāḥ bhidyete rūpanāmanī || 21 ||

Meaning: The attributes of (Pure) Existence, Consciousness and Bliss (Sat, Cit, Ānanda) are equally present in space (sky), wind, fire, water, earth, gods, men, animals etc. Names and forms mark them differently from each other.

Brahman equally pervades the five great elements (Pañca-Mahābhūta), animals, human beings, Gods etc. However, it is still detached from them. Insentient five great elements, primitive species such as insects, intellectually evolved species such as human beings are all limiting adjuncts (Upādhi, उपाधि) of Brahman.

Upādhi (limiting adjunct) is that, which pertains to a confined space of an object and helps to know that object. It separates the space of that object from the remaining space. E.g. the ear pinna is an Upādhi that helps in the cognizance of the ear sense organ, but itself stays separate from the organ. It is a differentiator (Vyāvartaka, व्यावर्तक) and it does not enforce its own characteristics on the ear sense organ.

Similarly, name and form are Upādhi of embodied soul. Name and form separate an individual soul from the Universal Soul i.e. Brahman. Names and forms may vary; however, their common substratum Brahman exists eternally.

Practicing Concentration on Ātman (Samādhi)

उपेक्ष्य नामरूपे द्वे सच्चिदानंदतत्परः ।
समाधिं सर्वदा कुर्याद् हृदये वाऽथवा बहिः ॥ २२ ॥

Upekṣya nāmrūpe dve Saccidānandatatparaḥ |
Samādhiṃ sarvadā kuryād hṛdaye vā'thvā bahiḥ || 22 ||

Meaning: One should become indifferent to names and forms, establish unwavering devotion in Brahman, and persistently practice concentration (on Brahman) within the heart (Antaḥkaraṇa, अंतःकरण) and outside.

Spiritual practice involves being aware about Ātman or Pure Consciousness in an uninterrupted manner. The intellect (Buddhi, बुद्धि) should practice this attentive awareness. Kena Upaniṣad says -

प्रतिबोध विदितं मतं अमृतत्वं हि विन्दते । (2.4)

Pratibodha viditaṃ mataṃ amṛtatvaṃ hi vindate |

- 'Every 'acquired knowledge' is based on the substratum of Pure Knowledge (Jñānarūpa Ātman).'

Even if no new knowledge is acquired from outside, Pure Knowledge exists eternally. One should remember this fact while learning anything new in day-to-day life. Instead of just pursuing the new topic of knowledge, one should focus and contemplate on the substratum of Pure Knowledge i.e. Ātman.

By being indifferent towards names and forms, one can turn his attention inward and focus on Ātman.

Every experience consists of two factors -

Experiencer - one who experiences.

Experienced - one that gets experienced.

Chāndogya Upaniṣad says -

सर्वं खल्विदं ब्रह्म । *Sarvaṃ khalvidaṃ Brahman* / (3.14.1)

- 'In reality, everything is Brahman.'

Thus, both the experiencer and experienced are Brahman. Inside (the experiencer) and outside in the world, there is only Brahman. But ordinary human beings do not realize that. To help us realize that everything (inside and outside) is Brahman, this text presents six techniques of Samādhi (meditation).

Samādhi is primarily of two kinds:

Internal Samādhi (within the heart / Antaḥkaraṇa) - It is practiced with internal objects (thoughts, desires etc.) or words, hence **Subjective** in nature. The techniques of internal Samādhi are used to realize that 'the **experiencer**' is Pure Consciousness (Ātman).

External Samādhi (outside the heart /Antaḥkaraṇa)- It is practiced with external objects (such as a photo, flame etc.) or words, hence **Objective** in nature. The techniques of external Samādhi are used to realize that everything in the outside world that is '**experienced**' is Pure Consciousness (Brahman).

The two types are further subdivided as follows:

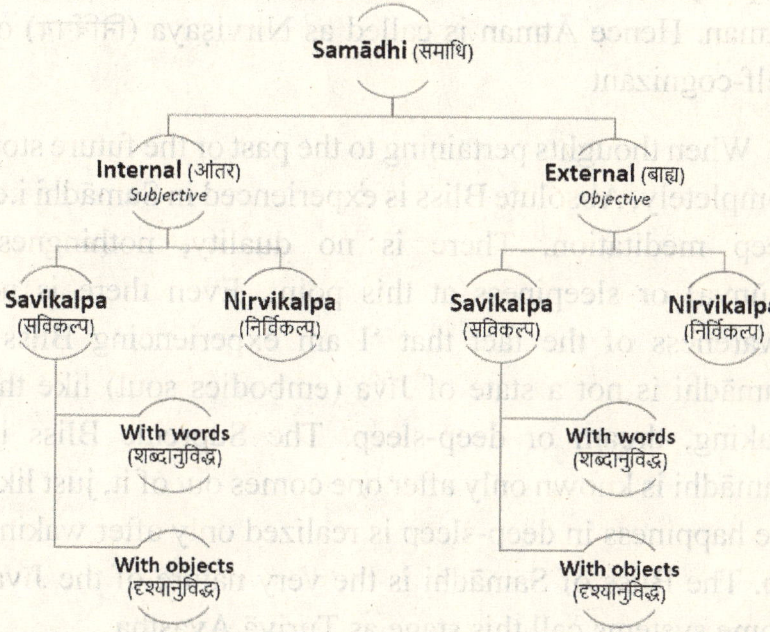

The practice of internal Samādhi (inside the heart) is to be done with the help of the doctrine of Vedānta. There is no reference to Aṣṭānga Yoga or Dhyāna Yoga (Gītā) here in these verses. Self-realization is the process of realizing that Ātman is the real Self or I. Ātman is attribute-less, formless and Self-cognizant. One that cannot be comprehended by routine way of gaining knowledge is called as Self-cognizant (Swasamvedya, स्वसंवेद्य). Ātman can be cognized only by being 'One' with it. Five sense organs cannot discern Ātman. Nine epistemically reliable means for gaining knowledge such as perception, inference, logic etc. (nine pramāṇas such as pratyakṣa, anumāna, tarka etc.) cannot comprehend Ātman. Hence Ātman is called as Nirviṣaya (निर्विषय) or Self-cognizant.

When thoughts pertaining to the past or the future stop completely, Absolute Bliss is experienced in Samādhi i.e. deep meditation. There is no duality, nothingness (Śūnya) or sleepiness at this point. Even there is no awareness of the fact that 'I am experiencing Bliss'. Samādhi is not a state of Jīva (embodies soul) like the waking, dream or deep-sleep. The Supreme Bliss in Samādhi is known only after one comes out of it, just like the happiness in deep-sleep is realized only after waking up. The Bliss of Samādhi is the very nature of the Jīva. Some systems call this stage as Turiyā Avastha.

To establish external concentration (outside the heart), one must learn to neutralize the favorable or unfavorable conditions around him. Human life is full of struggle and conflicts. The skill to resolve conflicts and stay equipoised must be acquired. A righteous and moral living is truly helpful for that purpose, as it helps the seeker to reduce the friction from his side. The world is not guaranteed to be harmonious or peaceful. One can only practice patience, control, tolerance (Titikṣā) and continue performing his daily duties in the best possible manner, while maintaining unconditional surrender to

Īśvara. At the same time, it is also necessary to stand up for oneself where necessary. The balance in practical life must be maintained. Rāmkrishna Paramhaṇsa gave a message – 'One should be able to hiss (like a snake) to protect himself, biting is not required!' St. Tukārāma said that a harmful scorpion must be killed with a footwear, even if it is sitting on the idol of a deity. A thoughtful, discriminative seeker gradually understands the subtleties in spiritual practice. Circumstances differ from person to person. They cannot be analyzed in a generalized manner. One must be aware of current events and circumstances, but not spend time in needless thinking about the world.

Internal Savikalpa Samādhi

सविकल्पो निर्विकल्पः समाधिर्द्विविधो हृदि ।
दृश्य-शब्दानुविद्धेन सविकल्पः पुनर्द्विधा ॥ २३ ॥

Savikalpo Nirvikalpaḥ Samādhirdvividho hṛdi |

Dṛśya-Shabdānuviddhena Savikalpah punardvidhā || 23 ||

Meaning: The internal Samādhi is of two different kinds - Savikalpa and Nirvikalpa. Savikalpa Samādhi is further divided in two types - One associated with objects and the other associated with words (Dṛśyānuviddha and Shabdānuviddha).

The internal Samādhi is divided into three kinds:

- आंतर दृश्यानुविद्ध सविकल्प (Āntar Dṛśyānuviddha Savikalpa) - Internal Savikalpa Samādhi with objects
- आंतर शब्दानुविद्ध सविकल्प (Āntar Shabdānuviddha Savikalpa) - Internal Savikalpa Samādhi with words
- आंतर निर्विकल्प (Āntar Nirvikalpa) - Internal Nirvikalpa Samādhi

The objective of the internal Samādhi is to help the practitioner realize that he himself is Pure Consciousness (Ātman or Dṛk).

In Savikalpa Samādhi, the 'practitioner' and 'the practice of concentration' are present distinctly from each other. There is no thought pertaining to the gross body or the world in this stage. In Nirvikalpa Samādhi, the 'practitioner' and the 'practice of concentration' both get dissolved into Pure Consciousness. There is only Pure Consciousness at this stage. The difference between Savikalpa and Nirvikalpa Samādhi is broadly like the one between 'desire to sleep' and 'actual state of deep-sleep'.

Internal Savikalpa Samādhi with Objects

कामाद्याश्चित्तगा दृश्याः तत्साक्षित्वेन चेतनम् ।
ध्यायेद् दृश्यानुविद्धोऽयं समाधिः सविकल्पकः ॥ २४ ॥

Kamādyāścittagā dṛśyah tatsākṣītven cetanām /
Dhyāyed driśyānuviddho'yam Samādhih Savikalpakaḥ //24//

Meaning: Desires in the mind (and other similar emotions such as greed, jealously etc.) are to be treated as (internal) perceivable objects. Meditate on Ātman (Pure Consciousness) as their Witness. This is called as Savikalpa Samādhi i.e. concentration on Ātman with the help of (internal) objects.

Ātman or Pure Consciousness is self-cognizant (Swasamvedya, स्वसंवेद्य) i.e. it can only be cognized by being One with it. Kena Upaniṣad describes Ātman with the verse -

यन्मनसा न मनुते । *Yanmanasā na manute* / (2-1-11)

- '(Ātman is that) which cannot be known by the mind, but the mind works on the substratum of Ātman.'

Bhagvad-Gītā says -

यो बुद्धेः परतस्तु सः । *Yo buddheḥ paratastu saḥ* (3-42)

- '(Ātman is that) which is superior to the intellect, which itself is superior to the mind and sense organs.'

Brahmasūtra says -

तर्काप्रतिष्ठानात् । *Tarkāpratiṣthānāt* (2-1-11)

- 'The intellectual logic has no place in the process of Self-realization i.e. the realization of Ātman.'

These verses state that one cannot meditate on Ātman with the help of the intellect or the five sense organs or the mind. However, it is possible to meditate on Ātman as a Witness to all internal thoughts or emotions.

The mind knows the presence of emotions such as craving, greed etc. Everyone understands his own desires. The subject of desire may be outside, but the mind knows the presence of desire internally. Ātman cannot understand the presence of a desire. Jīva (Embodied soul) does not cognize the presence of desire as well since the desire does not have a manifestation or a form (like an object). The doctrine of Vedānta says that desire, greed etc. are **Sākṣibhāsya (साक्षिभास्य).** They are the modifications in the mind, which are seen as being active only due to the presence of Ātman.

In this method of Savikalpa Samādhi, the practitioner should concentrate on the fact that he is the internal Witness (Sākṣī, साक्षी) to his own thoughts. Whenever a thought or desire is visible in the mind, the practitioner should perceive it as if it is an object different from himself. This helps to gradually become distant from one's own emotions, good or bad. The term 'visible' (Dṛśya, दृश्य) is used in a broad all-encompassing context here. Objects, which can be 'seen' with eyes are not the only ones that are 'visible'. Internal emotions that can be 'felt' are also termed as 'visible'. Desires, wishes, memories, daydreams, joys, sorrows, reactions, neutrality, win, loss, excitement, distress, enthusiasm, repentance, depression are all visible. Intellectual understanding is visible. All manifestations of the ego are visible. All wanderings of the mind are visible. Even the state of nothingness (Śūnya) in the meditation is visible i.e. it can be felt or experienced distinctly. All of these emotions are treated as objects in this type of Savikalpa Samādhi. One is not supposed to stop or redirect or fight or control his thoughts or emotions here. One is only supposed to practice being a Witness to his own thoughts and emotions, which are visible only to himself.

With more practice, one can understand the nature of the Witness. The 'I', in the thought 'I am the Witness' is not superimposed (Adhyasta, अध्यस्त), rather it is the substratum Ātman (Adhiṣṭhāna, अधिष्ठान). There is no other witness to this Witness. Without this assumption there will be impossibility problem / infinite loop (Anavasthā Doṣa, अनवस्था दोष) and the non-duality of Ātman will be refuted.

While contemplating deeply that 'I am the Witness', the practitioner suddenly experiences Samādhi.

विवृणुते तनुं स्वाम् ।

Vivṛṇute tanuṃ svāṃ / (Katha. Up. 2. 23)

- 'Ātman reveals its true nature only to the practitioner chosen by Ātman itself.'

In reality, Ātman cannot perform the action of revealing itself. It is non-doer, non-enjoyer (Akriya, Akrīḍa; अक्रिय, अक्रीड). It is eternally-attained (Nityaprāpta, नित्यप्राप्त). One should clearly understand the Vedānta doctrine and the context of this verse. Only a detached and genuine seeker may realize Ātman as his real Self. Ātman or Pure Consciousness is neither visible nor knowable. Ātman can only be realized by being One with it.

Worldly life involves the pursuit of Dṛśya i.e. visible objects. Spiritual life involves maintaining internal connection with Dṛk or Pure Consciousness, while living normal day-to-day life.

Internal Savikalpa Samādhi with Words

असंगस्सच्चिदानन्दः स्वप्रभो द्वैतवर्जितः ।
अस्मीति शब्दविद्धोऽयं समाधिस्सविकल्पकः ॥ २५ ॥

Asaṅgssacidānandaḥ svaprabho dvaitavarjitaḥ |
Asmīti shabdaviddho'yaṃ Samādhissvikalpakaḥ || 25 ||

Meaning: 'I am (Pure) Existence, Consciousness and Bliss, unattached, Self-effulgent and free from duality'. Being consistently connected with this thought is the second type of Savikalpa Samādhi with words.

In verse 24, the Savikalpa Samādhi is practiced by being the Witness to all internal objects (thoughts and desires). As one progresses in it, one can dissociate from the objects, and instead concentrate on the words, which describe the very nature of the Witness i.e. Ātman.

(Internal) Objects are useful only to create awareness that 'I am the Witness'. Once the awareness is established, the practitioner can drop the objects (emotions or thoughts) and focus on the nature of Ātman.

This verse mentions four specific words to contemplate on Ātman.

- **असङ्ग** (Asañga) - Unattached
- **सत्-चित्-आनन्द** (Sat-Cit-Ānanda),
  i.e. (Pure) Existence, Consciousness, Bliss
- **स्वप्रभा** (Svaprabhā) - Self-effulgent
- **द्वैतवर्जितः** (Dvaitvarjitaḥ) - Free from duality

Upaniṣads describe these facts in following verses -

- **असङ्गोह्ययं पुरुषः ।**
  Asañgohyayam Puruṣḥ / (Bru. Up. 4.3.15)
  - 'Unattached'
- **सत एव सौम्य इदमग्र आसीत ।**
  Sat eva somya idamagra āsit / (Chan. Up. 6.2.1)
  -'Sat i.e. Pure Existence is the primordial beginning of this Universe'
- **चेतनः चेतनाम् ।**
  Cetanaḥ cetanām / (Katha. Up. 5.13)
  - 'Cit i.e. Pure Consciousness'
- **आनंदो ब्रह्मेति व्यजनात् ।**
  Ānañdo Brahmeti vyajanāt / (Tai. Up. 3.6)
  - 'Ānanda i.e. Pure Bliss'

- तस्य भासा सर्वमिदं विभाति ।
  Tasya bhāsa sarvamidam vibhāti / (Katha Up. 5.15)
  - 'Swaprabhā i.e. Self-effulgent. Everything else is illumined (known) in the light of this Ātman.'
- एकमेवाद्वितीयम् ।
  Ekamevādvitiyam / (Chan. Up. 6.2.1)
  - 'Dvaitavarjita i.e. Free from duality'

The second type of (internal) Savikalpa Samādhi, involves continuous contemplation on Ātman with the help of these and similar texts. Practitioner should concentrate on thoughts such as - 'Ātman is completely detached (Asañga) from everything in the Universe. Ātman is Self-effulgent. Every object gets illumined (known) in the light of Ātman. Ātman is (Pure) Existence, Consciousness, Bliss. It is the only One, transcendental, eternal truth. There is nothing else but Ātman; I am Ātman (Pure Consciousness).'

The practitioner has to concentrate only on these or similar words from Upaniṣads and ensure no other words or thoughts arise in the mind. For this, he should have gained control on the mind and organs (Śama and Dama). He should have practiced abstinence and detachment. As the contemplation on these words grows deeper, the actual words take a back-seat and only Ātman remains in the thoughts. Gradually, the thought that 'I am Ātman' becomes prominent. The words of Upaniṣads and awareness of **I** become insignificant. Savikalpa Samādhi with words is said to be achieved when this state sustains for a while.

Internal Nirvikalpa Samādhi

स्वानुभूतिरसावेशाद् दृश्यशब्दानुपेक्ष्य तु ।
निर्विकल्पस्समाधिः स्यात् निवातस्थित दीपवत् ॥ २६ ॥

Svānubhūtirasāveshād dṛśyaśabdānupekṣya tu |
Nirvikalpassamādhiḥ syāt nivātasthita dīpavat || 26 ||

Meaning: Nirvikalpa Samādhi is that in which, there is steady realization of Ātman by being one with it. The experience of steady and complete absorption in Ātman is just like an unflickering flame of a light kept in a place free from the wind. All objects, words and sounds are dissolved in this stage.

Nirvikalpa means that, which has no desires, wishes, duality, differences etc. After consistent practice of Savikalpa Samādhi, one becomes ready (eligible) to practice Nirvikalpa Samādhi. A practitioner should first establish utmost stability in the (internal) Savikalpa Samādhi (with words), as described in verse 25.

For Nirvikalpa Samādhi, the text ('I am Ātman, I am detached, Self-effulgent, non-dual etc.') with which one is contemplating on Ātman, needs to be dropped as well. The (internal) objects and text are both completely relinquished here. This effort of relinquishing objects and text should be done with the subtle, awake mind (Sūkṣma, Sajaga Buddhivṛttī, सूक्ष्म, सजग बुद्धिवृत्ती). The subtle, awake mind needs to first stop all activities in the mind, surrender all spiritual practices, and then dissolve itself in the Pure Consciousness. After the mind is totally dissolved, Ātman, which is verily the nature of the Self is revealed. Attaining Nirvikalpa Samādhi is not a matter of practice or effort. It comes by itself. This mysterious experience is very personal. Only the practitioner who experiences it, knows it. It is inexplicable and incomprehensible by others. To talk about this experience is as incorrect as listening about it from someone.

Many definitions and types of Samādhi have been explained according to the Sampradāyas. E.g. Samprajñāta, Asamprajñāta, Vitarkānugata, Nādayoga, Rasānandayoga, Layasiddhiyoga, Bhaktiyoga, Rajayoga etc. Some of them may match partially to the types of Samādhi explained in this text. However, explaining them is not the prime objective here.

The concept of Samādhi in this treatise has been discussed with the help of the definition -

समाधियते यस्मिन अन्तःकरणम् इति समाधिः ।

Samādhiyate yasmin Antaḥkaraṇam iti samādhiḥ |

- 'One whose mind (Antaḥkaraṇa) is completely dissolved in Ātman is said to be in Samādhi.'

It is necessary to understand the theory of Vedānta behind Nirvikalpa Samādhi. The mind (Antaḥkaraṇa, अंतःकरण) is falsely superimposed on the substratum of Ātman. The superimposed mind dissolves in its substratum Ātman in Samādhi. Imaginary dissolves in the Absolute Truth (Satya). However, this Samādhi is not the same as deep-sleep (Laya, लय) or nothingness (Śūnya, शून्य). In both Nirvikalpa Samādhi and deep-sleep, the mind is dissolved and there is no duality at all. However, in deep-sleep, there is no knowledge of the Self, while in Nirvikalpa Samādhi, one realizes that Pure Consciousness is the real Self. Nirvikalpa transcends three Guṇās of Sattva, Rajas and Tamas. Ātman is Pure Knowledge, hence Nirvikalpa Samādhi is Pure Knowledge as well.

Samādhi cannot be experienced in a limited or a single body part. Some Sampradāyas ask to establish focus on the middle of the eyebrows, tip of the nose, center of the heart etc., which is fine in their own context. This text does not refute that. Some people see dazzling light, hear mystic sound (Anāhata nāda, अनाहत नाद), or experience their body growing exceptionally tall in the preliminary stages of Samādhi. That might be encouraging or motivating for practitioners. Some may even feel scared of leaving the physical body while practicing Nirvikalpa Samādhi. But such fear should be resolutely discarded. Jīva (embodied soul) leaves the gross body only according to his destiny (Prārabdha, प्रारब्ध). It is meaningless to feel skeptical about whether one is going to wake up before sleeping. It is equally meaningless to feel anxious about whether one is going come out of Samādhi before entering into it.

After attainment of Nirvikalpa Samādhi, ignorance (Ajñāna, अज्ञान) and its manifestations (Dṛśya) are permanently discarded. Practitioner becomes indifferent to insecurities, fear, dualities and limited thinking. Like waves that disappear in ocean, or ornaments that melt in pure gold, the mind (Antaḥkaraṇa) disappears in Ātman. In other words, false superimposition (Adhyāsa, अध्यास) disappears in its substratum (Adhiṣṭhāna, अधिष्ठान) i.e. snake disappears in the rope, or shining silver disappears in the sea-shell. Hence sage Sureshvaracharya says that, there is no need to repetitively study for Self-realization (Naiṣkarmyasiddhi). The practitioner realizes that he himself is the Pure Consciousness at this stage.

Now the following three verses describe the external Samādhi, which is divided into three kinds:

- बाह्य दृश्यानुविद्ध सविकल्प (Bāhya Dṛśyānuviddha Savikalpa) - External Savikalpa Samādhi with objects
- बाह्य शब्दानुविद्ध सविकल्प (Bāhya Shabdānuviddha Savikalpa) - External Savikalpa Samādhi with words
- बाह्य निर्विकल्प (Bāhya Nirvikalpa) - External Nirvikalpa Samādhi

The purpose of the external Samādhi is to help the practitioner realize that everything outside (of himself) that is experienced is Pure Consciousness (Brahman). He himself is One with that Pure Consciousness.

External Savikalpa Samādhi with Objects (Bādha-Samādhi)

हृदीव बाह्यदेशेऽपि यस्मिन् कस्मिंश्च वस्तुनि ।
समाधिराद्यस्सन्मात्रात् नामरूपपृथक्कृतिः ॥ २७ ॥

Hridīv bāhyadeshe'pi yasmin kasmiñshca vastuni |
Samādhirādyassnmātrāt nāmarūpapṛuthakkrutiḥ || 27 ||

Meaning: External Savikalpa (Dṛśyānuviddha, दृश्यानुविद्ध) Samādhi can be practiced with the help of any object. For that, name and form of an object need to be separated from Pure Existence (Sat or Brahman).

In verse 24, there is description of Savikalpa Samādhi with the help of an **internal** object such as as a thought or an emotion. This is the second kind of Savikalpa

Samādhi which can be practiced with any **external** objects such as a person, deity, photo, flame etc.

One thing is sure that the realization of Ātman does not take place through a medium of any person or object. Words or objects are not mediums, but they are used to in the process of discarding imaginary entities other than Ātman. In fact, the concept of entities other than Ātman is redundant, since Ātman is the only One non-dual principle. But we are habituated to the manifold life filled with many objects. The external Savikalpa Samādhi with objects is explained by keeping in mind this reality.

All external objects have -

Constant	Changeable
Existence (Asti, अस्ति) Cognizance (Bhāti, भाति) Likeability (Priya, प्रिय)	Name (Nāma, नाम) Form (Rūpa, रूप)

Existence, as we perceive, is always associated with names and forms. Names and forms are illusory (Māyic, मायिक) in nature. All worldly entities, and even elementary particles like Higgs-Boson may be said to be created from **Māyātron** (मायाट्रॉन). [*Note*: This term is coined by the Author.]

In this Samādhi, the practitioner should thoughtfully dissociate himself with names and forms of objects and concentrate on the 'Pure or Absolute Existence' common to all objects. Pure Existence is that, which exists irrespective of any person, object or entity. Objects, names and forms come and go, but Pure Existence is transcendental. It exists eternally.

Once the practitioner is able to focus on the Pure Existence that is constant in all objects, and dissociate himself from changing names and forms, it leads to Bādha-Samādhi (बाधसमाधी), which is Samādhi while working in day-to-day life. All saints, seers did enormous work while remaining in this Samādhi. Enlightened people experience the world just like other ordinary people, but internally they have a firm resolve that objects and their names and forms are illusory (Mithyā, मिथ्या). They see all worldly objects only as Pure, Absolute Existence.

External Savikalpa Samādhi with Words (Intermediate Samādhi)

अखंडैकरसं वस्तु सच्चिदानंदलक्षणम् ।
इत्यविच्छिन्नचिन्तेयं समाधिर्मध्यमो भवेत् ॥ २८ ॥

Akhanḍaikarasaṃ vastu Saccidānandalakṣaṇam |
Ityavichchinnachinteyaṃ Samādhirmadhyamo bhavet || 28 ||

Meaning: Brahman is (Pure) Existence, Consciousness, Bliss. It is homogeneous, eternal and has no divisions due to space, time etc. Uninterrupted contemplation on this thought is called as Intermediate Samādhi.

In verse 27, the external Savikalpa Samādhi is practiced by separating names and forms of all objects and focusing on Pure Existence common to all objects. Gradually, one can drop the external objects and focus on the words that describe the Pure Existence (Brahman). Objects are useful only for understanding that names and forms of objects are transient. Once that awareness is established, the practitioner can dissociate from the objects and focus on the (Pure) Existence, Consciousness, Bliss aspects of all objects.

This verse mentions four specific words to contemplate on Brahman. Seeker should understand the meanings of these words and delve deep into them -

- अखण्ड (Akhaṇḍa) - Undivided or indivisible
- एकरसम् (Ekarasam) - Homogeneous, monolithic
- सत्-चित्-आनन्द (Sat-Cit-Ānanda)
  - (Pure) Existence, Consciousness, Bliss
- अविच्छिन्न (Avicchinna) - Without any division

Upaniṣads describe these facts in following verses -

Brahman is all-pervasive, omnipresent & (Pure) Existence, Consciousness, Bliss (Sat-Cit-Ānanda).

- रसो वै सः ।

Raso vai saḥ (Tai. Up. 2.7)

- 'Brahman is the essence of the entire creation. It is full of Bliss.'

- नेह नानास्ति किञ्चन ।

  Neha nānāsti kiñcan (Bru. Up.)

  - 'There are no parts or divisions in Brahman. Other than Brahman, nothing else exists.'

- एकमेवाद्वितीय ।

  Ekamevādvitiya (Chān. Up. 6.2.1)

  - 'Brahman is verily the only One principle, without a second (entity).'

- वासुदेवः सर्वमिति ।

  Vāsudevaḥ saravamiti (Gītā. 7.19)

  -'One should uninterruptedly reflect that everything is essentially Vāsudeva (Lord Kṛṣṇa i.e. Brahman) in nature.'

- एकधातुर्द्रष्टव्यं ।

  Ekadhāturdraṣṭavyam (Chān. Up. 6.2.1)

  - 'Brahman has no differences, distinctions (Bheda, भेद) of any of the following three kinds -

  - **Self-difference** (Swagata Bheda, स्वगत भेद) - Within a fruit of apple, we find seeds, skin, pulp, stalk etc.
  - **Intra-difference** (Swajātīya Bheda, स्वजातीय भेद) - Apple and Kiwi are both fruits, but different from each other.
  - **Inter-difference** (Vijatīya Bheda, विजातीय भेद) - Apple is different from trees, stones etc.

No such differences exist in Brahman.'

The mind that contemplates on these verses naturally dissolves in the state of Samādhi. It is called as intermediate Samādhi because it is superior to the Savikalpa Samādhi explained in verse 28, but inferior to the Nirvikalpa Samādhi described in verse 29.

External Nirvikalpa Samādhi

स्तब्धीभावो रसास्वादात् तृतीयः पूर्ववन्मतः ।

एतैः समाधिभिः षड्भिः नयेत्कालं निरंतरम् ॥ २९ ॥

Stabdhibhāvo rasāsvādāt tritiyaḥ pūrvavanmataḥ |

Etaiḥ Samādhibhiḥ shadbhiḥ nayetkālaṃ nirantaram || 29 ||

Meaning: Supreme Bliss and tranquility is experienced when the mind dissociates completely from external objects and disappears in Ātman. One should uninterruptedly practice these six kinds of Samādhi.

Nirvikalpa means that, which has no duality of any kind. After consistent practice of Savikalpa Samādhi, one becomes ready (eligible) to practice Nirvikalpa Samādhi. A practitioner should first establish utmost stability in the (external) Savikalpa Samādhi (with words), as described in verse 28.

For this Nirvikalpa Samādhi, the text with which one is contemplating on Ātman (described in verse 28), needs to be dropped as well. The (external) objects and text about Brahman are both completely relinquished here.

In this Nirvikalpa Samādhi, everything that is 'this', 'that' or 'I' gets dissolved in Pure Consciousness (Ātman). Ātman pervades everything and everyone. There is no cognizance of past or future in this stage. Samādhi takes place in the present time. The practitioner experiences the Pure, Supreme Bliss of Ātman (Sarasa, सरस) in this Samādhi.

Rasa means nectar or essence. In this verse, it refers to the nature of Supreme, eternal Bliss of Ātman.

Tai. Up. (2.7) says -

रसो वै सः । रसं हि एव अयं लब्ध्वा आनंदी भवति ॥

Raso vai saḥ | Rasahyevāyam labdhvā ānandī bhavati ||

- 'Ātman is the essence of the entire creation. It is full of Bliss. The nectar of Ātman gives (everyone) Supreme Bliss.'

One feels happy after enjoying sense objects (eating favorite food, listening to good music etc.) and wrongly perceives that the happiness is a result of enjoying external objects. In reality, the mind (Antaḥkaraṇa, अंतःकरण) becomes quiet after enjoying sense objects. As a result of the quiescence of the mind, the eternally-available Bliss of Ātman manifests, which is the main reason for happiness.

The dualities of following kinds are obstacles for Samādhi –

- Attraction - aversion (Rāga-Dveśa)
- Superior - inferior
- Beautiful - ugly
- Auspicious - inauspicious
- Pious - impious
- Comfort - agitation
- Enthusiasm - boredom
- Attachment - detachment
- Cheerfulness - Whining
- Success - failure
- Friend - enemy
- Profit - loss
- Endearing - un-endearing
- Respect - disrespect
- Close - distant
- Clean - dirty
- Edible - nonedible
- Rich - poor
- Intelligent - foolish
- Fair - dark
- Religion - non-religion
- Justice - injustice
- Righteousness - non-righteousness
- Calmness - restlessness
- Praise - criticism

All these are manifestations of one pair of duality, which is good-bad (अनुकूल-प्रतिकूल). E.g. what is edible for one person may be nonedible for another.

If a practitioner is constrained by any of these dualities, he cannot practice Samādhi. The definitions of good (favorable) and bad (nonfavorable) change from time to time. Bhagvad-Gītā asks the seeker to maintain an equipoised state in all cases and situations. In the enlightened state, equipoise comes naturally.

People who deeply reflect on Ātman and stay detached from the everyday actions of the body are unusual and rare. The states of waking, dream and deep-sleep, wavering of the mind, good and bad experiences, are all parts of worldly life. They do not come in contact with the eternally detached (Asang, असङ्ग) Ātman.

असङ्गोह्ययं पुरुषः ।

Asaṅgohyayaṃ Puruṣaḥ / (Bru. Up. 4.3.15)

- 'Ātman or Pure Consciousness is completely unattached.'

All worldly activities are perceivable (Dṛśya). They get illumined by the light of Self-effulgent Ātman, so they are insentient in nature. When we look at all traits and events (good or bad) as only 'illumined', they don't create different reactions in the mind. Just the thought that they are 'illumined' and not 'Self-effulgent', can help us maintain equipoise under all circumstances.

Samādhi can be briefly summarized as -

- Internal Savikalpa Samādhi associated with objects & words, internal Nirvikalpa Samādhi (**Subjective**)
- External Savikalpa Samādhi associated with objects & words, external Nirvikalpa Samādhi (**Objective**)

These techniques of Samādhi should be practiced from the easiest to the hardest. The terms 'easy and hard' are relative and vary from person to person.

The State of an Enlightened Person

देहाभिमाने गलिते विज्ञाते परमात्मनि ।

यत्र यत्र मनो याति तत्र तत्र समाधयः ॥ ३० ॥

Dehābhimāne galite vijñyāte paramātmani |

Yatra yatra mano yāti tatra tatra samādhayaḥ || 30 ||

Meaning: One who has dissociated from the attachment to the body ('I am body' mindset) and realized that Ātman is the real Self, experiences (uninterrupted) Samādhi wherever his mind goes.

Identifying oneself with the body (I am body) is a form of ignorance (Ajñāna, अज्ञान). It disappears with consistent and steady practice of Samādhi. The practitioner realizes that Ātman is his real Self. He transcends the boundaries of physical body and the gross world in this process. However, the world doesn't magically disappear after realization of Ātman. The enlightened person continues to see everything around him like he did before. But he experiences Ātman everywhere as a result of his enlightenment. The thought that 'I am (Pure) Existence, Consciousness, Bliss' becomes his very nature. All attachments, concerns, worries, concerns about the world and body (Dṛśya) dissolve at this stage.

The world and body are transient in nature. The cycle of creation and destruction takes place continuously, which is unavoidable. In the body, new cells get created (anabolism) and old ones get destroyed (catabolism). There is more creation than destruction when the body is young. After a certain age, creation slows down, and destruction increases. This leads to old-age and finally death. Everyone is scared about death to some extent. 'I will die when the body dies. I will have to leave all that I have earned in this world' - these are the two main reasons for the fear in human life. Creation and destruction also take place continuously in the small world where a person lives. Family, house, business, relatives, power, success and fame come and go continuously. Both desired and undesired events take place in the world. E.g. people in combined families wish that the family be separated, and the family indeed breaks apart. Parents want their children to lead a happy married life, however, in some cases the marriage breaks apart. Blissful life is impossible if one thinks 'I am the body' and believes that the world is real.

Once the seeker has unwavering (Dridha, दृढ) and unalterable (Aparivartaniya, अपरिवर्तनीय) realization that Dṛk is his real nature, he becomes enlightened with the Pure Knowledge of the Self. He sees Pure Consciousness everywhere around him. All creations and destructions are illumined in the light of Pure Consciousness. He understands that objects and events are insentient and illusory (Mithyā) and stays unaffected by them.

The multiplicity and abundance in the world (Dṛśya) are very enticing in nature. People, nature, food delicacies, clothes, objects, travel destinations, vehicles such as airplanes, arts, sports are all captivating in nature. Besides these, power, wealth, success, fame and prestige are very attractive for most people. Comparisons, jealousy, competitions pollute the human life. A person who persuades only worldly objects, faces constant duality in the form of joys and distress.

One who constantly stays in reflective connection (Anusandhāna, अनुसंधान) with Dṛk becomes Pure Bliss himself. Ordinary people are unable to reflect on Dṛk most of the times. They are constrained by ignorance. People who strive to stay connected with Dṛk are desirous of liberation (Mumukṣu, मुमुक्षु). Those who have steadfast internal connection with Dṛk and continue performing regular activities in the outside world are enlightened people (Jīvanmukta, जीवन्मुक्त).

After Self-Realization

भिद्यते हृदयग्रंथिः छिद्यन्ते सर्वसंशयाः ।
क्षीयन्ते चास्य कर्माणि तस्मिन् दृष्टे परावरे ॥ ३१ ॥

Bhidyate hṛdayagranthiḥ chidyante sarvasañshayāḥ |
Kṣīyante cāsya karmāṇi tasmin dṛṣte parāvare || 31 ||

Meaning: After Self-realization, all knots (bondages) of the heart (Antaḥkaraṇa, अंतःकरण) are broken, all doubts are resolved and all Karmas (actions and their results) wear away.

This verse is taken as is from Muṇḍaka Upaniṣad (2.2.8). When knots are cut asunder, the person becomes free from bondages. Vāsanās in the mind (unfulfilled desires from past births) are known as Grañthi (ग्रंथी, fetters or bondages). Vāsanā is the very reason for a person to get into the life-death cycle. Vāsanā stays in the intellect (Antaḥkaraṇa, अंतःकरण). After Self-realization, the distinction between the intellect, Vāsanā and objects comes to an end. Vāsanā is insentient in nature. It is not related or attached to Ātman. Vāsanās pertaining to the body, objects, scriptures, people, children etc. are related to the world. They are illumined (known) in the light of Ātman. Katha Up. says -

कामा येऽस्य हृदिश्रिताः ।

Kāma ye'sya hṛdiśritaḥ / (2.3.14)

- 'Desires stay in the shelter of the mind (Antaḥkaraṇa, अंतःकरण).'

Thoughts such as 'I am body, I must live as long as possible, I need to collect many objects for my enjoyment, I should have deep knowledge of scriptures, and people should praise me', strengthen the Vāsanā and create knots (fetters) in the mind. They are broken only after the knowledge of Ātman.

When there is no awareness of Dṛk, the elements of triad (perceiver, perceived and perceiving) are experienced distinctly from each other. Even if people understand the process of perceiving, the real perceiver remains largely unknown.

Dṛk cannot be known unless scriptures or Sadguru explain it properly. Hence Dṛk is constantly a subject of curiosity, guesswork, assumption, ambiguity and apprehension. **Koham? Kathamidam Jatam?** (कोहम्? कथमिदम् जातम्?) – 'Who am I? How was this (world) created?' – These questions indicate curiosity. Being apprehensive about the world is also a form of curiosity. 'How is the world created? From where? When? Why?

Who created it? How long will it last?' - These questions are the right topics of the curiosity.

जन्माद्यस्य यतः ।

Janmādyasya yataḥ |

यतो वा इमानि भूतानि जायन्ते ।

Yato vā imāni bhūtāni jāyante |

Once we systematically learn meanings of these Śrutis and understand the meaning of 'Yasya' and 'Yato', the curiosity about the world is put to rest.

The gross body takes birth and consequently dies. Ātman is birthless and deathless (Aja, Amar). After realization that 'I am Ātman', all doubts about own body as well as those of others are completely eradicated.

The Karmas of Self-realized people work in the following manner -

Fresh new actions (Āgāmi Karma, आगामी कर्म) and the accumulated actions (Sañchiṭa Karma, संचित कर्म) do not produce any results. Prārabdha Karma (प्रारब्ध कर्म) is the set of actions, which have germinated and bore fruits, on account of which a person gets his present body. The body lasts so long as Prārabdha Karma continues to yield results. These results must be experienced and exhausted even by an enlightened person. The body of a sage continues to exist only due to Prārabdha.

Brahman is Parāvara (परावर). The word Parā indicates high i.e. cause and Avarā indicated low i.e. effect (Universe etc.). Brahman is all-pervasive and omnipresent, both in the cause and the effect. After realizing that 'I am Brahman' the Karmas wear away as described above.

The Samādhi described in Dṛk-Dṛśya Vivēka is different from the one in Ashṭānga Yoga. It does not involve just silencing the mind or putting a leash on its wandering nature (Cittavṛtti Nirodha, चित्तवृत्ती निरोध). It emphasizes more on the mind (Citta) dissolving into Ātman and being One with it. When a practitioner is able to reflect on Ātman (Dṛk) and the world (Dṛśya) as directed by Vedic doctrine and Sadguru, the Samādhi of Supreme Knowledge (Jñāna-Samādhi, ज्ञानसमाधी) is culminated.

Samādhi sustains only for a very few moments. Deep, focused chanting can help resurrect the Samādhi. Knowledge (of Brahman) should always be coupled with utmost, loving devotion to the God. Great saints like Kabira, Rāmdāsa Swāmi, Tulsidāsa, Eknātha Mahārāja, Sūrdāsa were excellent combination of Yoga, Knowledge and devotion. This is reassuring for all genuine seekers. At the same time, Sage Sureśvarācārya says that once the Knowledge of Brahman (as the real nature of the Self) is realized, there is no need to 'gain' that Knowledge repetitively over and over again (Naiśkarmyasiddhi).

Dṛk is the only eternal, transcendental truth. Others such as the perceiver (seer or Draṣṭā), perceived (Dṛśya) and sense of perception (Dṛṣṭi) are all illusory (Mithyā). They are perceived (known) only on the substratum of Dṛk. Dṛk is sentient. It illumines the other three factors, which are insentient, illuminable and transient in nature. Attachment to Dṛśya cannot lead to the ultimate objective of the human life, which is Pure, Absolute, Supreme Bliss.

Scriptures and saints recommend that we genuinely focus and consistently reflect on Dṛk. Being One with Dṛk is the epitome of a meaningful, elevated and triumphant human-life. This is the real gist of Dṛk-Dṛśya Vivēka treatise.

Meditative Refutation
of the
Four Bodies

Meditative Refutation of the Four Bodies

(Tanu-Catuṣṭaya-Nirasana, तनुचतुष्टयनिरसन)

[A special supplement for the readers of Dṛk-Dṛśya Vivēka.]

~ A Meditation Method in Vedānta ~

According to Vedānta, Jīva (embodied soul) has four bodies -

1. Gross body (Sthūla deha, स्थूल देह)
2. Subtle body (Sūkṣma deha, सूक्ष्म देह)
3. Causal body (Kāraṇa deha, कारण देह)
4. Supracausal body (Mahākāraṇa deha, महाकारण देह)

The four bodies are perceived (Dṛśya) on the substratum of Dṛk (Ātman or Pure Consciousness). The process of meditation described in this article helps for sequentially refuting each body in meditation and reach the ultimate stage of Self-Realization, where the perceived four bodies disappear in Dṛk and Jīva is unified with Brahman.

Samartha Rāmdāsa Swāmi has written a chapter named **तनुचतुष्टयनिरसन** (Tanu-Catuṣṭaya-Nirasana) in his spiritual treatise 'Dāsbodha' (दासबोध). It explains a process of Meditation based on the theory of Vedānta.

Ātman, the real Self, is said to be encapsulated by the four bodies. Ātman is Pure, Supreme and Eternal Bliss. In meditation, when the four bodies are refuted one-by-one, 'Ātman' as the real nature of the 'Self' is realized. It is an evolution from 'gross, corporeal existence' to 'Absolute, Pure Existence' that is eternally present. After meditative refutation of each body, Jīva becomes one with Ātman and Pure Bliss which is hidden as a 'supreme secret' gets revealed. Pure Bliss is also called as **Soliva Sukha** (सोलीव सुख), which means happiness unveiled by removing unnecessary covers over it.

St. Tukārāma Mahārāja makes an appeal to the God to enable him to realize Supreme Bliss. He says -

देवा आतां ऐसा करी उपकार। देहाचा विसर पडो मज।

तरीच हा जीव सुख पावे माझा। बरवे केशीराजा कळो आले॥

Devā ātā aisā karī upakāra | Dehāca visara paḍo maja |

Tarica ha Jīva sukha pāve mājhā | barave Keshirājā kalo āle||

- 'Oh God! Please help me forget the existence of my body, only then I will be able to realize the Supreme, Pure Bliss.'

Śri Samartha Rāmdāsa Swāmi guides all seekers to strive for transcending the four bodies. He says -

देहबुद्धि ते आत्मबुद्धि करावी। (Manobodha 163)

Dehabuddhi te Ātmabuddhi karāvī |

- 'Evolve from identification of the Self with body to identification of the Self with Brahman.'

This evolution involves removing the sheaths of four bodies on the 'Self' with a guided thought process. Scriptures and Sadguru provide us specific guidance to detach from body to experience the 'ever-existent' Bliss of Ātman.

There are two types of spiritual practices -

1) **Peripheral practices** (Bahirañga Sādhanā, बहिरंग साधना) such as fasting, pilgrimages, pious observances etc.
2) **Core practices** (Antarañga Sādhanā, अंतरंग साधना) such as -
   - Intent listening (Śravaṇa, श्रवण)
   - Contemplation (Manana, मनन)
   - Deep and constant thinking on the principle of Brahman (*Nididhyāsana*, निदिध्यासन).
   - Analysis of 'Tat and Tvam' words (*Tattvam-padārthaśodhana*, तत्त्वंपदार्थशोधन) along with Soham meditation.

Ātman cannot be realized with 'peripheral practices' irrespective of how meticulously they are done. Ādi Śaṅkarācārya says -

चित्तस्य शुद्धये कर्म न तू वस्तूपलब्धये । (Vivek. Chu. 11)

Cittasya śuddhaye karma na tū vastūpalabdhaye /

- 'Actions are needed only for purification of the mind. Ātman cannot be realized with any action.'

Selfless actions lead to purification of the mind (Citta-śuddhi, चित्तशुद्धि). Selfless worship with utmost love for the God (Upāsanā, उपासना) leads to quietening the mind (Cittaśānti, चित्तशांति). Pure, calm and stable mind is highly conducive for performing the practice of Tanu-Catuṣṭaya-Nirasana, which is an effective and extremely subtle core practice (Antaraṅga Sādhanā).

A seeker needs to be eligible (Adhikāri, अधिकारी) to conduct the practice of Tanu-Catuṣṭaya-Nirasana. He should gain adequate knowledge of the nature of a 'body' from the Vedānta scriptures and complete the necessary groundwork.

The ignorance about the nature of the Self exists on four levels -

1. Firm conviction that 'I am body', when in fact 'I am Brahman'. This is most rigid form of ignorance.
2. 'The body is mine'. This is a weaker form of ignorance as compared to the first one.
3. 'I am not body'. This is the weakest form of ignorance.
4. 'I am Ātman'. Theoretical or intellectual conviction is categorized as a very mild ignorance since it is in the realm of awareness. Ātman (Pure Consciousness) is beyond the realm of both awareness and unawareness.

When these four stages of ignorance are crossed, one can attain Self-realization. A person who strongly identifies himself with the body is more like an animal from the perspective of Vedānta. Even if such a person leads a very prosperous worldly life, he is still considered unfortunate and miserable. On the contrary, a person is considered fortunate if he has done the prescribed groundwork for spiritual pursuit in a meticulous manner.

Both ignorance and 'liberation from ignorance' are imaginary in nature. Liberation means Mokṣa. Being liberated is the very nature of each Jīva.

Tukārāma Mahārāja says –

बंध मोक्ष शीण तुका म्हणे । *Bandha mokṣa śīṇa Tukā mhaṇe ||*

- 'The ideas of bondage and liberation are both burdensome.'

Liberation is possible only if the bondage is present for real. How is it possible to be liberated from an imaginary bondage? However, so long as we experience imaginary bondages of 'I am body' and 'the world is real', liberation (Mokṣa) should be considered a real goal. It must be pursued with persistent spiritual practice. Tanu-Catuṣṭaya-Nirasana should be conscientiously practiced for that purpose.

It is necessary to understand the concept of **Vṛttī** (वृत्ती) before proceeding further. Any modification in the state of mind (Antaḥkaraṇa, अंतःकरण) is termed as **Vṛttī** (वृत्ती).

Conceptually, Vṛttī can be seen as a wave or ripple in the original unperturbed state of mind.

For most ordinary people, mind is always wandering. A Vṛttī is always at work. Presence of Vṛttīs in the mind is an obstruction in the path of enlightenment. While meditating for Tanu-Catuṣṭaya-Nirasana, Vṛttīs need to be properly channelized and eventually silenced to realize Ātman. The process of silencing Vṛttīs and refuting four bodies is discussed in detail below.

Gross Body (Sthūla Deha, स्थूल देह)

For refuting the gross body in meditation, Vṛttī needs to detach from gross body and engage in the subtle body that comes next in order.

Detachment from the gross body needs extensive preparation. The practitioner should first learn to reduce affinity and involvement in worldly matters. Identification of the Self with the body compels us to pamper the body, spoil it, indulge in its desires and cater to all its cravings. As a result, the mind gets attached to the body.

Vṛttī can easily detach from the gross body when mineness is reduced from it. Engaging and pledging the gross body to sublime, noble causes reduce the feeling of mineness. It is also important to use proper discrimination to serve rightful causes for this purpose.

Dedication to worldly pursuits (e.g. winning a gold-medal in Olympics or mastering a musical instrument etc.) helps in detaching from body to some extent. But the worldly matters are ultimately corporeal, so such detachment is not helpful in spiritual pursuit. For Self-realization, body should be assigned for doing increasingly altruistic causes. It should laboriously toil to serve the society, religion, righteousness, God or Sadguru. The more evolved and noble cause one chooses for dedicating the gross body, the more he gets detached from it. Such detachment is profound, unwavering and conducive for meditation.

Indian culture has established a system that encourages devotion to increasingly more sublime causes as one grows and evolves. Vedic doctrine has proposed four 'Āśramas (आश्रम)' or 'phases of life' that assist people of all age groups to prepare themselves for a definite purpose in life. It prescribes dedicating gross body for -

- Serving Sadguru and gaining knowledge in Brahmacaryāśrama (ब्रह्मचर्याश्रम)
- Fulfilling duties, responsibilities towards family, society, nation and serving elders in Gṛhasthāśrama (गृहस्थाश्रम)
- Sincerely pursuing spiritual studies in Vānaprashthāśrama (वानप्रस्थाश्रम)

Execution of duties in this manner leads to detachment from gross body by the time one reaches the last stage of Sañyāsāśrama (संन्यासाश्रम). Even though, the system of adapting formal Āśramas is not so practical in today's age, seekers can adapt to modern times and perform the prescribed actions in given circumstances. Those who live benevolent and self-effacing life easily progress in the spiritual path. Rituals such as going to pilgrimages, fasting, pious observances are meant only to weaken the sense of 'mineness' in body.

Selfless dedication is a peripheral practice to reduce affinity in the body. There are deeper core practices that help in refuting gross body in meditation.

Vedānta states that Gross body is made up of the five great elements (Pañca-Mahābhūta, पंचमहाभूते) -

- Earth (Pṛthvī, पृथ्वी)
- Water (Āpa, आप)
- Fire (Teja, तेज)
- Wind (Vāyu, वायू)
- Space (Ākāśa, आकाश)

The elements are mixed together in specific proportions with the process of **Quintuplication** (Pañchīkaraṇa, पंचीकरण) to form the gross body. The five elements are insentient in nature. So, the gross body is insentient as well. By itself, the gross body cannot perform any activity. It functions only when impelled by

Jīva (embodied soul). Jīva takes birth, acquires the body for some time and leaves the body at the time of death. So, the gross body is transient in nature. The seeker can meditate upon the thought that he has been given the gross body only for a limited period. It is necessary to detach from it, since it is not permanent in nature.

The strong conviction that 'I am body' is called as Dehādhyāsa (देहाध्यास). Adhyāsa means deceptively seeing presence of one object instead of the other. Jīva is originally 'Brahman' but mistakenly sees himself as a 'body'. In meditation, 'I' and 'my body' need to be separated from each other with the help of Vivēka. The simple logical statement 'whatever is **mine** is not **me**' can help in this process. E.g. If the house is mine, I am not the house. If the shirt is mine, I am not the shirt. Similarly, if the body is mine, I am not the body.

One can also think that the body is given to him by Īśvara, so it does not belong to him. Īśvara owns the body. One can meditate upon the thought that the body needs to be given back to its owner at the time of death hence it is not right to nurture affinity in it.

These simple, yet powerful thought-processes can truly help the practitioner refute the gross body in meditation. Self-realization is possible only for those rare, courageous, brave seekers who can reduce their affinity and detach from the gross body.

Subtle Body (Sūksma Deha, सूक्ष्म देह) -

Subtle body is made up of 19 elements, which are:

- 5 sense organs (Jñanendriyas, ज्ञानेंद्रिये)
  - Ear (Śrotra, श्रोत्र)
  - Nose (Ghrāṇa, घ्राण)
  - Eyes (Chakṣu, चक्षु)
  - Tongue (Jihvā, जिह्वा)
  - Skin (Tvak, त्वक्)
- 5 action organs (Karmendriyas, कर्मेंद्रिये)
  - Hands (Pāṇi, पाणि)
  - Feet (Pāda, पाद)
  - Mouth (Vāk, वाक्)
  - Rectum (Pāyu, पायू)
  - Genitals (Upastha, उपस्थ)
- 5 Life Forces (Prāṇas, प्राण)
  - Prāṇa (प्राण)
  - Vyāna (व्यान)
  - Apāna (अपान)
  - Udāna (उदान)
  - Samāna (समान)
- Antaḥkaraṇa Catuṣṭaya (अंतःकरण चतुष्टय)
  - Mind (Manas, मन)
  - Intellect (Buddhi, बुद्धि)
  - Memory (Citta, चित्त)
  - Ego (Ahaṅkāra, अहंकार)

Sense and action organs which are mentioned in the subtle body are activating centers of their gross body counterparts. Out of these 19 elements, refuting Antaḥkaraṇa Catuṣṭaya is the most important and difficult aspect. This article mainly focuses on refuting the mind (Manas, मन) in meditation.

The Vṛttī or the 'state of mind' that goes after worldly objects is called as '**gross mind**' (Sthūla Buddhivṛttī, स्थूल बुद्धिवृत्ती). The 'gross mind' is extrovert as it invariably runs outwards for enjoying various pleasures.

The Vṛttī or the 'state of mind' that strives for refuting the four bodies during meditation is called as '**subtle mind**' (Sūkṣma Buddhivṛttī, **सूक्ष्म बुद्धिवृत्ती**). It is introvert as it strives to search for Pure Bliss of Ātman. 'Subtle mind' needs to be kept awake, alert and functioning until all four bodies are refuted. For effective practice, it is important to carefully cross the four obstacles in meditation -

1. Laya (लय) -

The seeker may fall asleep in meditation while refuting each of the four bodies. This is a negative trait. It is usually a result of laziness, too much laborious work or sleepiness. A tired body naturally induces lethargy. To avoid Laya, the practitioner should eat light meal and get adequate rest before meditation. Early morning is the best time since it prevents sleepiness during practice.

2. Vikṣepa (विक्षेप) -

Vikṣepa means 'wandering of the mind'. The extrovert nature of the mind is the main reason for Vikṣepa. Gross mind (Sthūla Buddhivṛttī, स्थूल बुद्धिवृत्ती) is so indomitable that it constantly runs outwards to worldly subjects. The nature of mind is such that only one Vṛttī (वृत्ती) can stay in it at one time. Continuous functioning of the powerful 'gross mind' doesn't allow 'subtle mind' to focus and meditate.

There are three techniques to overcome this obstacle. One is to put a resolute, forceful leash on the 'gross mind' and prevent it from wandering outside. Second is to think about the transient nature of worldly objects and convince the mind to stay away from impermanent happiness that they offer. Third technique is to gradually distance oneself and calmly watch the activities of the mind as a witness. The mind gradually stops wandering and becomes calm when one practices these techniques.

3. Kaṣāya (कषाय) -

The mind thinks incessantly about people or objects that it loves or hates the most. These imprints on mind obstruct the meditation. The mind remembers events in past or worries about future. Constant internal thinking, memories, daydreams or future-plans form the obstacle of Kaṣāya. It can be avoided with proper discrimination between real and unreal aspects of life (Vivēka).

4. **Rasāswāda** (रसास्वाद्) -

When earlier obstacles are crossed, the seeker may feel very happy and linger in that intermediate happiness as a result. This is the fourth obstacle in meditation named **Rasāswāda** (रसास्वाद). However, this is a 'negative happiness', which is experienced due to the absence of worries, sorrows or wandering of the mind. It is important to consciously recognize and cross this hurdle during practice.

To overcome these obstacles and proceed in meditation, the practitioner should conduct his day-to-day activities with rigorous discipline. Meditation is not meant to be just one-hour mechanical practice each day. The entire life-style needs to be modified and made conducive for it. The mind should be trained to stay calm and focused throughout the day (Nididhyāsana, निदिध्यासन). If it wanders for ~23 hours, then it will not be possible to quieten it just for some time meditation. One should be alert before and after meditation as well.

The mind has been often equated with a monkey, since both are restless in nature. The mind (Manas, मन) is created from **'wind element'** (Vayūtattva, वायूतत्त्व), so it wanders all the time. But a street performer who organizes monkey-plays for entertainment keeps the monkey completely under control. He holds one end of the leash on monkey and mandates it to jump, dance, walk and perform all other possible tricks. Similarly, the 'subtle mind' (Sūkṣma Buddhivṛttī, **सूक्ष्म बुद्धिवृत्ती**) should take charge of the 'gross mind' (Sthūla Buddhivṛttī, **स्थूल बुद्धिवृत्ती**) in Tanu-Catuṣṭaya-Nirasana.

The practice of Śama-Dama is highly effective for this purpose. **Śama** means 'controlling the mind', and **Dama** means 'controlling the organs'. Śama is first while Dama is second in order. If the mind is controlled from desires, organs will not run for fulfillment of those desires, so there will be no need to practice Dama i.e. restraint of organs.

The interdependence of controlling 'mind and organs' (Śama and Dama) can be illustrated with an example. When 'eyes' see a delicate, beautiful rose, 'hands' promptly pluck it due to an impulse to acquire the rose. The sequential process of 'watching', 'desiring' and 'acquiring' occurs extremely quickly, involuntarily and almost imperceptibly. Eyes look at the rose. The mind makes a wish (Saṅkalpa, संकल्प) to acquire it, and conveys information given by eyes to the intellect. Unfulfilled subconscious desires (Vāsanā, वासना) are imprinted in the intellect. If rose can fulfill a Vāsanā, then the intellect decides to acquire it. The decision of the intellect is then conveyed to hands via the mind. Ultimately hands pick up the object and acquire it.

This process explains the fact that 'mind' acts as an intermediary between 'intellect' and 'organs'. The mind conveys information gathered from 'sense organs' to the 'intellect'. It also conveys the decision from 'intellect' to the 'action organs'. So, if the mind is trained not to crave for objects, then the organs will not work in that direction. The infinite loop of desires and their fulfillment will be terminated. There will be no need to practice Dama.

Desires are generated in the mind in two ways -

1. **Internal generation of desire:** Desire gets generated in the mind (Antaḥkaraṇa, अंतःकरण) due to unfulfilled subconscious desires (Vāsanā, वासना) from many past births. E.g. some people intrinsically love to travel to outdoor places, while some love to just sit at home and watch TV. These innate desires are governed by Vāsanā, which reside in the intellect (Buddhi).
2. **External generation of desire:** Desire gets generated due to outgoing sense organs. E.g. while roaming in shopping malls, suddenly we see new costumes, which fascinate us. We buy them impulsively without any prior desire or planning. The new objects are first sensed (seen, heard, smelt, touched) by the organs. The mind conveys information about new pleasures to the intellect. The intellect decides to acquire new object, if it aligns with Vāsanās and conveys the

decision to organs via the mind. The organs act to acquire the object as dictated by the intellect.

Whether the desire for objects is generated internally or externally, the mind acts as an intermediary in both cases. So, with control of one factor i.e. mind (Śama), intellect, organs and the entire subtle body is eventually restrained.

But it is an arduous task to control the flickering, turbulent, strong, obstinate mind. St. Jñāneśwara says-

जे इंद्रिया आणि बुद्धि । माझारिलिये संधी ।

रजोगुणाच्या खांदी । तरळत असे ॥ (Dnyā. 13.104)

Je indriyā āṇi buddhi | Majhāriliye sandhī |

Rajoguṇācya khāndī | Taralata ase ||

Rajoguṇa (Rajas Guṇa) is the base foundation of the mind. It is the very reason, which makes the mind obstinate, turbulent and wanderer. When Rajoguṇa is dominant, the mind continues its two-way travel from 'intellect' to 'organs' and vice-versa. For controlling the mind, Rajoguṇa itself needs to be attacked. If Rajoguṇa is weakened, the mind cannot wander, stray or jump around, Vāsanā do not demand for more worldly pleasures and organs remain silent since they don't need to work towards fulfillment of desires.

To debilitate Rajoguṇa, it is important to keep a diligent tab on meals, movements, behavior, conduct and conversations that strengthen its presence.

Spicy meals, heavy desserts or bizarre delicacies nourish Rajoguṇa. Superfluous reading, daydreaming, laughing at trivial jokes, wearing a wide variety of clothes, fancying jewelry, being lured by cosmetics and perfumes are some of the manifestations of Rajoguṇa. It is a part of the culture of pretentiousness and pompousness. Rajoguṇi people also try to bedeck their families, friends and relatives to put up an ostentatious display and impress others. The culture that endorses lavish traits, glamorous living with plush interiors and rich furniture can never become conducive to true spiritual practice. Luxurious places may look great from outside, but they are completely futile and ineffective for genuine seekers. Superficial spiritual practices done delicately without putting the body through any hard-work, are counterproductive. They give fake happiness and prevent the seeker from Self-realization. The real spiritual pursuit requires a great degree of effort, hard-work and commitment. Only grueling, focused and consistent practice serves in the best interest of seeker and leads him to Mokṣa.

It is also natural for seekers to get influenced by the conduct, behavior, habits, conversations and thoughts of other people. The three Guṇās play an important role in this context. Śri Samartha says about three Guṇās -

सत्त्वगुणे भगद्भक्ती । रजोगुणे पुनरावृत्ती ।
तमोगुणे अधोगती । पावती प्राणी ॥

Sattvaguṇe bhagvadbhaktī | Rajoguṇe punarāvṛttī |

Tamoguṇe adhogatiī | Pāvatī prāṇī ||

- 'Sattva Guṇa impels devotion to the God, Rajoguṇa impels getting into life-death cycle, and Tamas Guṇa impels total deterioration.'

For a seeker, it is necessary to carefully distinguish between good and bad company, seek good company and avoid bad company. Man is a social animal. He cannot stay in solitude for long. So, it is necessary to strive to seek the company of virtuous people. Sages and saints impel us to contemplate about the true nature of the God and the Self. They show the way to lead sublime, exemplary life. They inspire us to tread the path of upliftment. Their divine internal energy influences us. Spiritual practices proceed in a focused and consistent manner in their company. Saints are personification of Brahman; hence their grace and blessings help us make significant progress in our journey. Śri Jñāneśwara says -

परी संतांसवे बैसता । योगज्ञानी पैसता ।

गुरूचरण उपासिता । वैराग्येसी ॥

Pari santānsave baisatā | Yogajñyānī paisatā |

Gurucaraṇ upāsitā | Vairāgyesi || -

- 'By keeping company of sages and saints, gaining knowledge of yoga, serving at the feet of Sadguru and following the path of renunciation - one can realize Ātman.'

Most people innately crave for worldly objects. Indulging in pleasures comes naturally to them. In the company of other Rajoguṇi people, one's Rajoguṇa becomes even more fierce and forceful. Tamoguṇi and Rajoguṇi friends are considered detractors since they regress the seeker and ruin his spiritual pursuit, so their company should be strictly avoided. Sattva Guṇi acquaintances should be consciously acquired. As Sattva Guṇa becomes dominant, Rajas and Tamas Guṇa become weak naturally. They stay in a suppressed state.

Thus, by monitoring meal intakes, movements, behavior, conduct and company, the support of Rajoguṇa is removed from the mind. Unending desires in the mind are reined in. Both external and internal impulsions for fulfilling desires come to an end. The mind (Manas) stops wandering. With that, the other two elements of Antaḥkaraṇa i.e. memory and intellect (Citta, Buddhi) are quietened, and consequently the fourth element of ego (Ahaṅkāra) also gets silenced. Organs, which work under direction of the mind, stop their work, since they do not get any commands from the mind. When the subtle body is trained in this manner for entire day, it becomes easy to refute it during meditation.

Apart from the practice of Śama-Dama and debilitating Rajoguṇa, there are deeper core practices that help in refuting subtle body in meditation.

Subtle body is made up of the five great elements (Pañca-Mahābhūta, पंचमहाभूत), which are insentient in nature. So, the subtle body is insentient as well. By itself, it cannot perform any activity. It functions only when impelled by the Reflected Consciousness (Cidābhāsa, चिदाभास) in Antaḥkaraṇa. Every-day during deep-sleep, one automatically forgets the subtle body since it dissolves in the 'causal body'. The seeker can learn nuances of this theory and deeply meditate upon the thought that the subtle body is insentient and transient in nature. So, it is necessary to detach from it and refute it to realize the real Self.

It is relatively easy to detach from gross body and refute it. However, it is extremely difficult to detach from mind. Most people strongly identify themselves with the thoughts, ideas and activities of the mind. In meditation, 'I' and 'my mind' need to be separated from each other with the help of Vivēka. The simple logical statement 'whatever is **mine** is not **me**' can again help in this process, just like it helped in the refutation of the gross body. E.g. 'If the mind is mine, I am not the mind. So, let the mind wander wherever it wants. Let the mind be agitated, angry, happy, excited or worried. The real I will just watch it as a witness.' This thinking is immensely beneficial in meditation. As one watches the activities of the mind, it stops wandering and gradually becomes calm. The same thought-process can be applied to silence other elements of the subtle body such as Prāṇa, intellect, ego etc. This simple, yet powerful thought-process can help the practitioner detach from the subtle body in meditation.

Once subtle body is refuted, the prior gross body is naturally forgotten.

Gross and subtle bodies are the two main bondages that connect us to the world. Freedom from these two bondages, helps to dissociate from the surrounding world. Learning to refute the 'causal body' is the third stage.

Causal Body (Kārana Deha, कारण देह)

When the 'gross mind' (Sthūla Buddhivṛttī, स्थूल बुद्धिवृत्ती) is refuted, only the 'subtle mind' (Sūkṣma Buddhivṛttī, सूक्ष्म बुद्धिवृत्ती) continues its work. The 'subtle mind' reaches a thought that, 'all elements are discarded. Nothing needs to be put aside now. Everything is very calm, still and quiet'. Since there are no thoughts about the surroundings, 'subtle mind' becomes one with this silence. The stage where it revels in this tranquility is called as the 'stage of nothingness' (Śūnyāvasthā, शून्यावस्था). This is called as the 'causal body' (Kāraṇa Deha).

The practitioner is disconnected from the world but not yet One with Ātman in this stage. Worldly thoughts do not arise, and the contemplation of Ātman does not begin. There is an intermediate state of stillness. The 'subtle mind' (Sūkṣma Buddhivṛttī, सूक्ष्म बुद्धिवृत्ती) experiences this joy of stillness and mistakes it as the 'Pure Bliss of Ātman' or 'Ātmānanda'. It takes a pause and stays still. Due to ignorance (Ajñāna), it mistakes this experience as being One with Brahman. Śri Samartha has written a verse for seekers who get stuck in this intermediate state -

इकडे दृश्य तिकडे देव | मध्ये शून्यत्वाचा ठाव |
तया प्राणी मंदबुद्धिस्तव | ब्रह्म म्हणे ||

Ikaḍe dṛśya tikaḍe deva | Madhye śūnyatvācā ṭhāva |
Tayā prāṇi mandabuddhistava | Brahma mhaṇe ||

- 'On one side there is Brahman or the God, on other side there is the visible world. In between there is nothingness (Śūnya, शून्य). Senseless, foolish people call it Brahman.'

This is an extremely fragile and a subtle stage where seeker can be deceived. This negligence does not let the seeker reach the ultimate Bliss of Ātman. What is experienced here is illusory happiness, not the real one. It is called as the 'illusion of Bliss' (Ānandāvabhāsa, आनंदावभास).

A seeker is supposed to take clear guidance from his Master or Sadguru about the stage of 'nothingness' in meditation. If it has been assimilated properly, the seeker will remember his Guru's guidance and words. Sadguru says, 'You are neither body, nor mind, nor prāṇa. Likewise, you are also not nothingness. You are that (principle of Brahman).' The 'subtle mind' recollects the guidance and starts contemplating again, 'If I am experiencing nothingness, who illumined that? How did I learn about the existence of Śūnya? There is a substratum on which I am able to comprehend nothingness. That substratum is ever-existent knowledge, also known as Ātman. I am that Ātman. Soham (Sahā-Aham - I am that).' When the 'subtle mind' (Sūkṣma Buddhivṛttī, **सूक्ष्म बुद्धिवृत्ती**) starts intensely focusing on Soham, Soham, it transcends the causal body at the same time, and enters the last supracausal body.

<u>Supracausal Body</u> <u>(Mahākārana Deha, महाकारण देह)</u>

When the 'subtle mind' enters the realm of Soham awareness, the causal body gets discarded. This fourth stage is called as Supracausal Body (Mahākāran Deha) where all three gross, subtle and causal bodies are completely forgotten. The 'subtle mind' (Sūkṣma Buddhivṛttī, सूक्ष्म बुद्धिवृत्ती) deeply meditates on Soham. While deliberating on Soham (I am that Brahman), Vṛttī gradually starts reveling in that consciousness and reaches very close to a distinctive, unusual happiness. It luxuriates in this Bliss. So much so that it forgets 'Aham' or I. What remains is only 'Sahā' or that Ātman which is

Absolute Knowledge and Supreme Bliss. When Vṛttī becomes One with Brahman, it also forgets separate awareness of 'Sahā'. In this very moment, the supracausal body ceases to exist i.e. the 'subtle mind' completely disappears in its own nature i.e. Ātman (Pure Consciousness). It transcends the realms of both awareness and un-awareness. There is no awareness of any of the four bodies or surroundings. Mind reaches the 'unmani' state (where mind ceases to be the mind). Jīva unifies with Ātman. What remains is 'Keval-Ātman' - one and only Ātman. The state when Citta disappears in Pure Consciousness is called as Samadhi. Jīva becomes completely one with Sat-Cit-Āṇanda Brahman. There is only unparalleled Bliss in this stage. This same state is known by various names - Anubhūti, Ātmānubhūti, Ātmadarshana, Ātmasthiti, Ātmasākṣātkāra, or Soliva Sukha.

Jīva does not have its own separate existence after the four bodies are refuted in meditation. So, the experience of being one with Ātman cannot be described. Neither Jīva, nor mind, nor vāni (speech organ) exist in this stage. Upaniṣad says an intriguing verse while trying to describe this ultimate stage of non-duality -

यतो वाचो निवर्तन्ते अप्राप्य मनसा सह । (Tai. Up. 2.4.1)

Yato vāco nivartante aprāpya manasā saha |

- 'The mind and vāni turn back from it since they are unable to grasp or describe it.'

Kena Upaniṣad says about this stage -

यन्मनसा न मनुते येनाहुर्मनो मतम् ।

तदेव ब्रह्म त्वं विद्धि नेदं यदिदमुपासते ॥ (1.1.5)

Yanmanasā na manute Yenāhurmanomatam |

Tadeva Brahma tvam viddhi nedam yadidamupāsate ||

- 'Brahman cannot be comprehended by the mind, but it is Brahman that gives the mind its thinking capability.'

Brahman can neither be comprehended by the mind, nor seen with eyes, nor heard with ears, nor smelt with nose, nor touched with skin. But, Brahman is the substratum on which all activities take place. All four bodies and their elements are eliminated when Jīva is unified with Brahman. The mind cannot contemplate about it; it dissolves in Ātman on the substratum of Ātman itself. It becomes one with Ātman very gradually, almost imperceptibly. The 'rough and tough' approach or 'fast-track' method does not work here. Persistent efforts are needed only until activities of the four bodies are completely silenced. After that, Jīva becomes one with Ātman in a very serene, peaceful manner.

When four bodies are meditatively refuted, the ever-existent Bliss of Ātman (Soliva Sukha) manifests itself. There is no need to change places, or do special rituals, or make or break anything to attain this ever-existent Supreme Bliss. Ātmānanda i.e. Pure Bliss is our very nature. Only with the grace of Sadguru can we reach this last stage of grace of Ātman, where it reveals itself.

Sadguru can make his disciple experience the perpetual Bliss of Ātman by the way of 'transmission of spiritual energy' (Śaktipāta Dikṣā, शक्तिपात दीक्षा). However, this momentary experience is just like a highlight. It convinces the seeker that Eternal Bliss truly exists. It is an enticement that makes him crave for that Bliss. He starts practicing for meditative refutation of the four bodies with even more commitment, hope, faith and resilience.

Self-realization needs the expert guidance of Sadguru. Enlightenment that comes as a result of his guidance is eternal. Hence, every seeker should seek the loving grace of Sadguru and pursue the spiritual path meticulously to attain the Pure, Supreme Bliss of Ātman.

Find more information about other books and lectures by the author **Dr. Shrikrishna Deshmukh** –

http://vedantbhaskar.org
http://www.shrikrupaprakashan.com/

- Select Hindi and English Translations at - http://vedantbhaskar.blogspot.in